Grief

Grief

Surviving the Storm After Someone You Love Has Died

MICHAEL S. THOMPSON

proving press

Copyright © 2020 by Michael S. Thompson

Book Design and Production:
Columbus Publishing Lab
www.ColumbusPublishingLab.com

Cover artwork by Gina Femrite. All rights reserved.
www.gina-femrite.pixels.com

All rights reserved. This book, or parts thereof,
may not be reproduced in any form without permission.

LCCN: 2019917872

Paperback ISBN 978-1-63337-340-2
Hardback ISBN 978-1-63337-385-3
E-book ISBN 978-1-63337-341-9

Printed in the United States of America

1 3 5 7 9 10 8 6 4 2

CONTENTS

INTRODUCTION	7
Chapter 1: How the Crow Flies	9
Chapter 2: The "Why" Question	17
Chapter 3: Do We Have Guilt or Regret?	27
Chapter 4: There's No Place Like Home	33
Chapter 5: What Should I Do with Belongings?	47
Chapter 6: What Is Journaling and Can It Help Me?	59
Chapter 7: Why Can't I Take Off My Wedding Ring?	71
Chapter 8: Surviving the Holidays	83
Chapter 9: Building a New Life	103
Chapter 10: Dating Again	111
Chapter 11: Who Is Elaine?	121
ACKNOWLEDGMENTS	131
ABOUT THE AUTHOR	133

Introduction

WHEN MY WIFE DIED, life as I knew it instantly changed. My existence seemed to have been ripped away from this world. I felt disconnected from the universe. No matter where my body was, my mind was detached from the present and in a dark, lonely place. Even though my body was on earth, I felt like I did not exist here. My stomach had a nervous feeling that I had never before experienced in my whole life. I felt an internal pain that was so intense I believed it came from my soul itself.

I could not believe my wife was dead! I remember thinking, *How can this be happening? Is this real, or am I having a bad dream?* This was the worst possible thing that could have happened. Our lives together were good, and we had plans for our future—this was not supposed to happen to us! Then a cold dose of reality hit me like I was being stabbed. There was no *us*. My wife was gone. I would never be able to talk to her again. She would never be coming home.

I will tell you something I have never admitted until now: I was afraid, and I wanted her back. But I was powerless to do anything to alter the horrible circumstances I had found myself in.

Within these pages, I have shared personal aspects of my life and how I worked through my grief. I am confident that you will find something in this book to help you. Perhaps you will gain a new perspective on an issue you are struggling with. I hope this book will be the lighthouse that helps guide all those who read it out of their storm of grief and back to a normal, happy life without fear, pain, regret, self-blame, loneliness, or never-ending grief.

When someone you love dies, it is the worst thing that could happen to you. But no matter how awful things may seem, eventually you will be okay. However, this is going to take some time. You will need to work persistently to make your life better again. You must have strength, courage, and hope. Getting through your loss may be the hardest thing you have ever had to do. But you can do it! Moreover, as you read my story, there will be times of deep sorrow, happiness, triumph, and failure. You will read things that will make you want to laugh and cry. When you are done reading, you may discover that doing so has helped you find the hope in your heart that you need to start creating a new life for yourself. The journey to rebuild your shattered life will be painful. As you press on through your pain, you will realize you have more strength and courage than you ever could have imagined.

You *can* overcome your loss, so do not give up! Have faith and believe that someday you will feel normal and happy. My prayers are with you. May this book be one of the tools that helps your broken heart begin to heal.

How the Crow Flies

MY WIFE, ELAINE, had some health issues and had survived a heart attack as well as developed chronic obstructive pulmonary disease (COPD). Although COPD is a serious lung disease, Elaine was managing her illness well. She was living a normal life and even working a full-time job. Everyone knew she would be alive for many more years. However, occasionally she would have some trouble breathing due to her COPD.

Early on a Sunday morning in March of 2009, I woke up and immediately noticed Elaine was not in bed—neither one of us ever got out of bed that early on a Sunday. So I went to look for her. I found her in the living room where she was having trouble breathing. Often when this happened, she would use her inhaler and eventually her breathing would return to normal. Because of this, my wife did not want to run to the hospital every time she had trouble breathing. However, because she'd had a heart attack several years earlier, we were never certain if her difficulty breathing was due to the COPD or something more serious.

Her inhaler was not helping this time, and things actually seemed to be getting worse. I was very worried and kept asking her if she wanted to go to the hospital. As she was pacing back and forth, taking periodic breaths with her inhaler, Elaine kept saying, "Let's wait ten more minutes." Enough time had gone by that I knew we needed to go to the hospital, but she was in denial and was refusing to go. She walked to the bathroom and almost fell to the floor but caught herself on the sink. I'd had enough of this ridiculous procrastination. In a stern voice I said, "That's it! We are going to the hospital right now!"

All she could reply was, "Okay." I took hold of her arm and we immediately started walking to the car in silence with only the clothes on our backs. We did not stop for anything. I did not even lock our front door, as I knew that would slow us down by a couple of seconds.

I drove fast, but made sure our vehicle did not jerk or spin its tires in any way as I did not want to alarm Elaine. I did not want her to know how worried I was! After a few minutes on the road, we started talking about what could be wrong. I told her everything was going to be fine, which made Elaine a little less distressed. She said she felt like her breathing was better, but I could not tell any difference.

Our small-town hospital was approximately seven minutes away, with the capability of flying a patient to one of the major hospitals very fast. During my employment in corrections, I was once required to ride with someone who was being flown to a larger, better-equipped hospital.

In the middle of this situation, fearing my wife could die, my mind began to recall an old saying I was told as a child: *The fastest way to get anyplace is to travel the way the crow flies.* This meant to travel cross-country in a straight line from point A to point B, flying overtop of things, and not stopping for or going around obstacles.

The medevac helicopter not only transports patients the way the crow flies, but it travels at an average speed of 120 miles per hour. I felt better knowing this, just in case my wife needed to be taken to another hospital.

When we got to the hospital, the doctors and nurses were very professional, but their faces showed a concern that was usually not noticeable. They did blood work and an EKG; both came back normal. However, because Elaine was having so much trouble breathing, they wanted to do a test to see if a blood clot had developed close to her lungs.

We were so relieved when that test came back normal too. Elaine was placed on oxygen and admitted into the hospital for observation. Her doctors believed her breathing trouble was caused by a cold that had turned into a slight case of pneumonia, but that she should recover with proper care and rest. The situation got even better when we were told Elaine would probably be discharged from the hospital the next day. However, the next day when they removed the oxygen, she still had some trouble breathing, so she was not able to go home. Nonetheless, we expected her to be discharged as soon as her body could maintain the proper oxygen level without the oxygen tank.

Each day we were disappointed when we were told she needed to stay another day. She had only been in the hospital three days, but I started to become increasingly worried. I was going to the hospital to check on her twice a day, both before and after work. I thought about calling in sick and staying with her, but she did not want me to do that. I was still worried even though she was not in the intensive care unit. I was starting to wonder if the doctors had overlooked something.

All of my fears went away when I arrived at the hospital one morning and Elaine was out of bed and had been walking around the entire hospital floor. She looked much better and was having an enjoyable conversation with her sister and nephew. The doctor also told her that she would be discharged in a day or two, but she might need to temporarily be on oxygen. Elaine was thrilled with this good news! All of us thought she was going to be okay. I left the hospital grateful that my wife seemed to be getting better.

When I returned to check on her later that night, she looked terrible and was having pain in her stomach. We asked to speak to the doctor, but we were told the doctor was gone and would not return until the next morning. I asked the nurse numerous questions about my wife's condition. The nurse gave us some reasonable explanations as to why Elaine was feeling worse. We were told that my wife's abdominal pain was being caused by gas. In order to relive her pain, the nurse had given her some medication and then checked Elaine's vital signs, which were fine. Logically I should have stopped worrying, but I just felt that something was very wrong. I wanted to do something, but I was trapped in a situation that was out of my control. As the hospital did not really enforce visiting hours, I stayed with Elaine a while longer. When it started getting late, she insisted I go home and try to get some sleep since we were both exhausted.

As promised, I called my wife when I got home. She asked me to hold the phone to the ear of her cat so she could tell him goodnight. The cat seemed to recognize her voice, and I think he missed her, and I knew Elaine missed him too. That cat was almost like one of her children. We talked a few minutes, and Elaine said she was feeling much better. She did not want me to come to the hospital so early the next day, because we were not sure what time the doctor would be making his rounds. I knew my wife was concerned about me and could tell I was tired and worried. So I agreed with her just so she would not be worried about me. I told her I loved her, we said goodnight, and I hung up the phone. Then I set my alarm because I was planning on being at the hospital early so I could personally talk with her doctor.

I had been sleeping on the couch in the living room because I could not sleep without Elaine in our bed. I was not getting much sleep either as I lay awake with all kinds of thoughts running through my mind. I was considering going to the hospital and sitting in the room with Elaine until the next morning when the doctor appeared for his rounds.

I have always had a tendency to worry excessively in certain situations, so I tried to think everything through rationally because I did not want to overreact. The nurse had told me that Elaine's vital signs were good, and the staff suspected she was feeling worse only because she had indigestion. She was not in the intensive care unit, and she had even been out of bed and walking around the hospital earlier. Taking all of this into account, I calmed down and decided to wait and go to the hospital in the morning. But I still had an overwhelming feeling that something serious was wrong. There was, however, really nothing I could do until I could speak with the doctor. So I did the only thing I could do: I got on my knees and prayed to God. I asked God to please protect my wife and help her get better.

After I prayed, I was still worried, but I was so exhausted that I laid my head on the pillow and fell into a deep sleep. The ringing of the phone woke me up, and I thought I had been asleep only a few minutes, but actually four and a half hours had gone by. The time was only a little after five in the morning, and no one would be calling me that early in the morning. I was terrified the call would be from the hospital. I was afraid to answer, my stomach was in knots, and I picked up the phone, hoping the call was a wrong number. My fear become a reality—the call was from the hospital. I was told that my wife had taken a turn for the worse and I needed to get to the hospital as soon as possible. I asked what was wrong over and over again, but the person would not tell me, saying only, "You need to get here right now!"

In a panic I pleaded, "I am on my way! You get my wife to one of the bigger hospitals where they can help her!"

The reply was, "We are working on that."

Then I called my father, who lived next door, to let him know what was happening. My father offered to drive me, and as we pulled out of the driveway, I was completely horrified at the thought of losing my wife. My dad tried to calm me down on the drive to the hospital. He said, "With the advances in modern medicine, a lot of times they can save people who are close to death." Although the circumstances looked bad, after listening to the pep talk from my father, I had a positive outlook and was holding onto the hope that she would be okay.

When we arrived at the hospital, we parked as close as possible to the entrance and ran inside. I told the receptionist who I was. She made a phone call and asked us to take a seat. Within a few minutes we were taken into a private room. A doctor told me that my wife had vomited and the vomit had gone into her lungs. The doctors tried to save her, but Elaine had died. At that moment

I felt an emptiness inside me. My whole world had been destroyed in a matter of seconds.

When my wife Elaine died, a part of me also died. A piece of my soul had been ripped away. I felt afraid and lost. I could not imagine my life without Elaine. I literally felt like I was dying from a broken heart. How was I ever going to be able to go on without her?

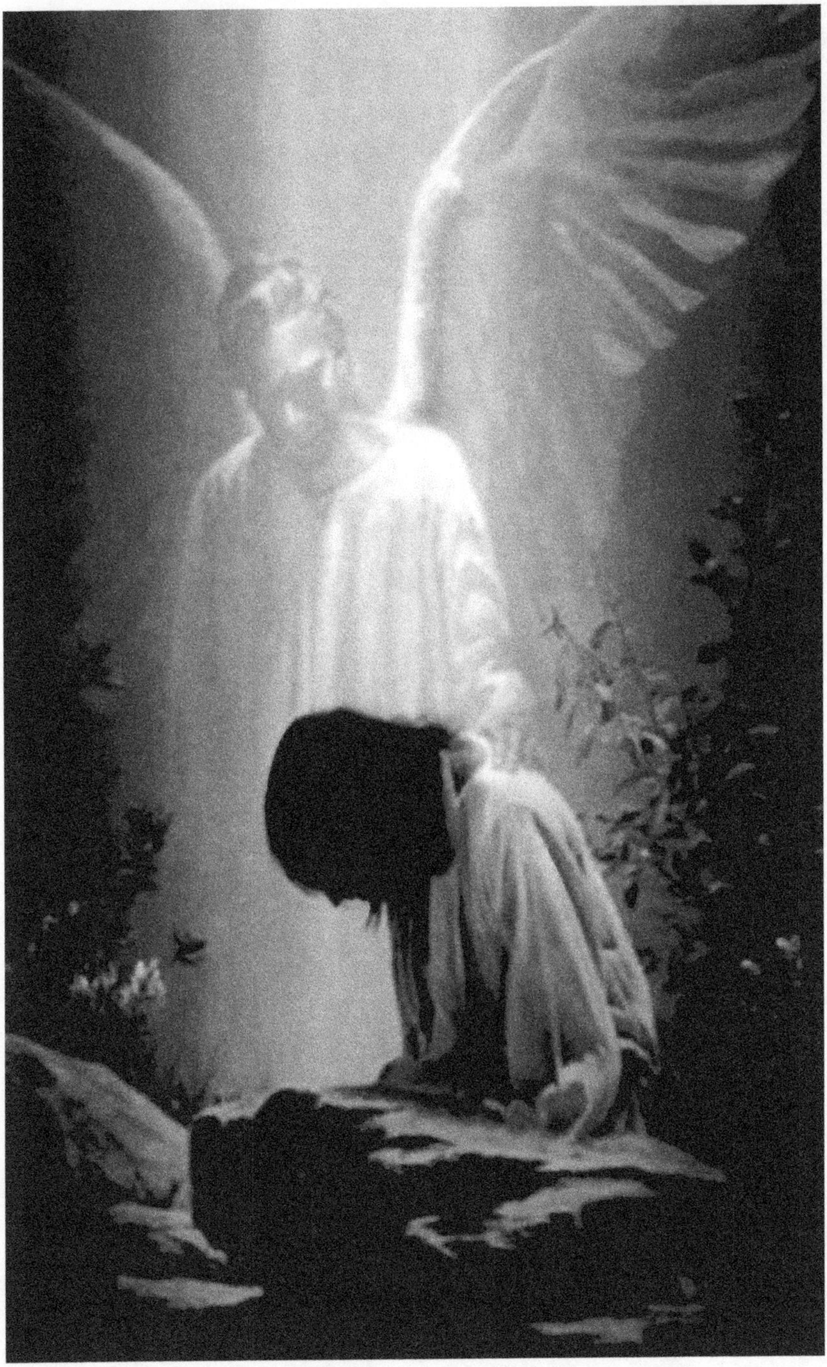

The "Why" Question

A LOT OF US who have lost a loved one are haunted by a question that infects our minds like a plague: *Why? Why did my loved one die?* We all know the medical reasons. Maybe it was a heart attack, cancer, some other disease, a car accident, or some other tragedy. That's not the part of the *why* question that lingers in our minds, waiting to relentlessly hurt us. The toughest part is wondering, *Why did this terrible thing have to happen? Why did I have to lose my loved one?* This person's death was not in our plans. Even if the person had been ill for some time, we were not prepared for the way the death would affect us. If the person was terminally ill, the why becomes, *Why was there not a miracle through which my loved one was the only person who got better?*

This one-word question is the beginning of many other questions. *Why me? And why now?* There are so many *why*s that people ask themselves depending on the individual circumstances. I believe it all comes down to wanting to understand and make sense of what has happened. We have been hurt terribly and are so heartbroken that it feels unbearable. We want answers to questions there are no answers to, questions like the following:

- Why did my loved one have to die so young?
- Why did my loved one have to die after retiring?
- Why couldn't my loved one have lived to see a child graduate?
- Why couldn't my loved one have lived to see the first grandchild born?
- Why did my loved one have to suffer with a sickness?
- Why did my loved one die so unexpectedly?
- Why did I never get to express my love one last time?

I have heard people say all these things, and the list just goes on and on. No matter what milestone in life we are at, we want more time with our loved one, so we ask why that person is not here for the next important point in our lives.

I believe some *why* questions help keep us stuck in grief, especially when we insist on wanting to know why life has dealt us such a tremendous blow. I was very angry that life had cheated my wife and me. I could not let that question go; I demanded an answer, and so do a lot of other people. I have seen people in grief groups struggle with constantly bringing up the *why* question as it relates to them. I had convinced myself that if God, a higher power and creator of the universe, would just tell me why my wife had to die, I would understand and my pain would go away. I think, for many people, finding an answer that is acceptable to them as to why in the grand scheme of things their loved one had to die does help take away some of the pain. At least it allows them not to feel like they and their loved one have been duped out of precious time.

People of strong faith will focus on their religious beliefs and Bible scriptures. I have heard these people say, "Everyone has a set time to be born and a set time to die." They will find serenity in seeing some positive outcomes in future occurrences and credit them to their loved one's death, especially things based on the spiritual aspect of people's lives, such as other family members or friends who have started attending church after the loss. Sometimes people find refuge in thinking that the death was more merciful than living in agonizing pain, or that at least their loved one was not here to suffer through some hardship that took place after the passing.

Death makes people think about things like destiny and their own immortality. Do things just happen, or are they destiny? How long do we have? The year my wife died, there had been some previous deaths at work. After my wife died, I saw several coworkers suddenly decide to retire, including one who had stated many times that he was going to work three more years.

I believed I was given some special signs from God, and from my wife, to help me with my grief. To be quite frank with you, this brought up another question for me: *Why me?* I did not attend church on any regular basis; I had been there maybe twenty times in my whole life, and I was forty-five years old when she died. There were some people in one of the grief groups I attended who could quote every verse in the Bible word for word. So I guess I should have felt truly fortunate for the privilege of receiving some special signs. And I did! But I was really hoping for one more. I wanted to know why she had to die, and I was waiting for God to tell me in a dream, or in some way that I would understand.

The grief group I was meeting with had been taken over by the pastor's wife. She was a very nice lady, and I believe her intentions were good when, in an attempt to comfort me, she said, "I think I know why [your wife died]." I was thrilled to hear this! When I asked her why, she said that before she could tell me, she wanted to make sure she was right. I took the comment to mean that she had been given a sign from God but wanted time to reflect. Believing that God had delivered a message to me through her that would clarify my blurred mental state, I waited patiently. However, after a month I could wait no longer. I finally insisted she tell me what God had revealed to her.

Her answer was a huge shock to me. I was expecting that God had sent her a message directly. What she told me was that she believed Elaine had died at this time because it was destiny that I would come to the grief group there at her church and become a Christian. She went on to say how great it would be if I brought all nine of my grandchildren and they too became Christians. So her explanation of why my wife had died was that it was God's way of introducing all of our grandchildren to Christianity.

Well, that was not why! When I heard her say this, I was at a total loss for words. I sat there stunned. I knew she was a nice lady and meant well, but I was a little bit angry with her. At the same time, I understood that this was just her way of thinking. In a somewhat strong demeanor, I replied in three words: "That's not it!" Then I said them again, shaking my head back and forth. I do not think she expected that reaction from me. I told her that seven of the grandchildren lived hundreds of miles away, so there was no way I could take them to church, and the two who did live close to me already went to church with their other grandparents. She looked flabbergasted, and I think a little embarrassed, but she realized I had wanted a specific answer from God Himself.

I drove home after the meeting very disappointed, and for the next week I felt even more like I would never be okay again. After a few days of major depression, I was finally able to get my state of mind back to the point where I was in my recovery prior to the devastating wrong explanation I had been given as to why my wife had died. However, I went on beating myself up for a long time, feeling like I was getting a little bit nearer to a state of insanity each day. I just could not let my mind accept what had happened. So I kept thinking, *Why did she have to die?* But every time I thought this or said this out loud, there came a mixture of many emotions: sadness, hopelessness, anger, emptiness, and the social alienation from what I perceived to be a normal life. I started to realize that whenever I was thinking or saying, "Why did she have to die?" I was feeling about as despondent and depressed as one could possibly get.

Fortunately, I had friends from my work and the grief groups I attended whom I could call when I was feeling this way. Also, my daughter-in-law, sister-in-law, and a friend I had jokingly nicknamed Watson (the sidekick of the famous fictional detective Sherlock Holmes) were often there to comfort me in critical moments. I also talked with a grief counselor.

You may be wondering how all this pertains to the *why* question. This *why* question is extremely dangerous and a huge obstacle. When we are fighting to recover from a deep, dark, lonely place during times of sorrow, starting to ask yourself, "Why did my loved one die?" only brings a more intense feeling of sadness. This can lead us to feel that we are in a bottomless abyss with no hope of finding our way out. In these moments I started thinking that there was no reason to go on existing.

If you are like I was and just cannot seem to let this *why* question go, for your own physical health and mental health you are going to have to find an answer.

Have you ever tried to reword the *why* question in a way that puts what you are feeling into the question? That might help you find a solution. Let me give you an example of my own rewording. Remember that we are all different with distinct feelings and thoughts. Consequently, each of us will reword the *why* question with our own feelings and thoughts.

My original question was, *Why did my wife have to die?* Now I can add on to the end of that original question this list of the following statements, because that was how I was feeling:

Why did she have to die because . . . ?
- I am all alone!
- I have no one to love, and no one will love me!
- I am being punished but did nothing wrong to deserve this!
- I have had another bad thing happen to me in my life.
- I prayed to God and asked for my wife to get better.
- I asked for God's help and He did not help!
- I have been denied love by destiny or even God Himself!
- I now live a life that has been destroyed!
- I will never have any happiness in my life ever again!

You may have noticed in my rewording of my *why* question that every feeling begins with the word *I*. I came to the realization that the *why* question was not only about how my wife's death affected her, but also about how her death affected me. More specifically, the question was about how I was feeling about her death and how it could impact my future.

A lot of those feelings were fueled by the grief and were not necessarily true. Nevertheless, those types of feelings and thoughts can really make the death even harder to accept. Basically, I was not only unable to accept that she had died, but I was also feeling sorry for myself and feeling like life had betrayed me. But I am not going to be hard on myself for feeling that way, or be condescending and point a finger of shame at you. What I am going to do is tell you something that might help you put the *why* question behind you once and for all. I am going to give you the answer I came up with to the *why* question...

The answer to the *why* question is that there is no answer! If there is such a thing as destiny, then destiny's plan is a secret! You're not going to know the final plan or reason now. If your loved one's death was God's plan and God has not told you why by now, it's the same thing—God is keeping the reason a secret. If you do not believe in destiny or God, consider this: in life, sometimes bad things just happen.

What helped me to put this *why* question behind me was that every time I would start thinking, *Why did she have to die?* I would just remind myself that I was never going to know the answer and it was pointless to keep asking myself! Then I forced myself to just think about something else. I know this is easy to say but not easy to do. For me, doing something like this is just about impossible. However, I became so frustrated and sick of not getting an answer that my anger gave me the ability to push those thoughts out of my mind. Although this helped me, it allowed me to get the *why* question out of my mind only temporarily. However, after some time had passed, I found that the *why* question popped into my thoughts less and less, and as time went by, it finally just went away. For me this took about a year and a half.

I want to share something with you that I discovered eight years after my wife died. Even though I had accepted her death and stopped asking myself why she had to die, when I learned about Japanese kintsugi, I felt a calmness inside my entire body. An inner peace that I had never felt before started to accompany my acceptance of her death. Kintsugi is a five-hundred-year-old art form of

Grief

fixing broken pottery by mixing lacquer with gold, silver, or platinum. The philosophy behind this is to recognize the history of something by repairing it in a way that does not hide the damage but rather incorporates the damage into the object. I have seen bowls and vases like this, which were so absolutely beautiful I could not bring myself to look away. The gold-filled cracks created a new and unique design that captivated me. Kintsugi emphasizes the importance of the history of what was once broken. The Japanese believe that when something has been damaged, it does not become repulsive but magnificently beautiful. Like a broken bowl, you have been damaged—your heart has been shattered! However, you have not been broken beyond repair. A vase or bowl can be fixed, and so can you. Try to have hope and not feel like life has betrayed you. No one has a flawless life; everyone will have some horrible things happen.

I once heard this quote:

"Every next level of your life will demand a new you."[1]

I think another appropriate quote would be this one by Ernest Hemingway: "The world breaks everyone; afterward, some are stronger at the broken places."

In order to become that new version of yourself, sometimes it takes being broken. So perhaps there is a plan for your future. But you have to choose whether you are going to let the death of your loved one destroy you, or whether you are going to put your broken heart back together. If you choose to fight through this pain, you will become a more insightful and understanding person because of what you have suffered. Just like Japanese kintsugi fills the cracks in a

---

[1] Sean Buranahiran, "Be Proud of Your Scars [Original Video] (kintsugi) – จงภูมิใจในบาดแผลของคุณ," August 25, 2017, YouTube video, 2:32, https://youtube/wG2MUeVixao.

broken vase with gold, you will begin to fill the cracks of your broken heart with gold—not 14-karat gold, but the gold of personal growth, which has an even greater value.

The repaired vase is never the same. It is no longer the same vase, but now is stronger, more valuable, and more unique; the vase becomes spectacular. It is now one-of-a-kind. The vase is now a new version of what it once was. Like the vase, you will become a new version of yourself. This might take some time, even years, but when you finally become the new you, there is no telling what life, destiny, or God might have planned for you. You might find yourself living someplace you never dreamed you would ever live, doing something you never dreamed you could ever do, overcoming a fear that you have had forever, traveling someplace you never would have gone, accomplishing something you never thought possible, or making a huge difference in someone's life. Some of these things have happened to me, and I have seen them happen for other people who have experienced a loss as well.

Remember that as long as you keep questioning and refuse to accept your present life, you will not be as focused on the things that are beneficial to your recovery.

I do not want you to think that after I stopped questioning and accepted the fact that my wife died, my grieving just stopped, because it did not. However, we all have to find an answer to the *why* question that is acceptable to us in order to be able to move on.

I hope there was something in this chapter that will help you put the *why* question behind you.

Do We Have Guilt or Regret?

WHEN SOMEONE WE LOVE DIES, we may feel guilty about certain things that have happened. We may be blaming ourselves for stuff that is not really our fault. Even if some of us did things that were wrong, rather than forgiving ourselves, we let the guilt eat us up inside. Guilt and regret are not the same, but sometimes we cannot distinguish between the two.

Guilt is when we are totally responsible for doing something wrong, and we feel bad about what happened. Regret is feeling sad or disappointed over something that has happened, such as a missed opportunity or wishing there had been a different outcome to a situation. Often we say to ourselves, "If only I had known what was going to happen, I would have done something different." This is regret, not guilt! Things we regret are not necessarily our fault, but yet we may blame ourselves even though we are not the ones who are responsible. We might be blaming ourselves for our loved one's death. For example, we may be thinking, *If only I had known how to do CPR, my loved one might be alive.* In our grief we overlook the fact that we did everything we possibly could have done; after all, a lot of what happens in life is completely out of our control.

If we could see into the future, very few things would ever go wrong in our lives. We certainly would not let our puppy run out into the yard if we knew that, on that day, our dog was going to dig under the fence and run away. Nor would we have driven down a certain street if we knew a kid playing baseball was going to hit a home run, sending the ball right at the car and cracking the windshield. We may regret driving down that particular street, but we realize the broken windshield is not our fault. For those we love, our job is always to protect and keep them safe. Therefore, our expectations of ourselves can be unrealistic at times when it comes to our loved ones. Unfortunately, none of us have super powers. So as long as we have done everything in our means to make things better, we have nothing to feel guilty about.

People can also regret certain aspects of their relationships. In every relationship there will be disagreements and heated arguments. When a person we love has passed away, we may recall not only the good times but also some of the bad times. We may wish we had handled the situation differently or even avoided the conflict completely. But no matter how much two people love each other, they are not going to get along all the time! This is normal in every relationship. An argument requires two people. It takes two to tango.

Elaine and I both had good moral values, and we were old-fashioned in our way of thinking. Neither one of us cheated, hit anyone, lied, or called each other names. Our marriage was very good! But don't think our life together was a make-believe fairy tale with no struggles. We occasionally had arguments in our everyday life; at one point I was not sure our marriage was going to survive.

When we first got married we had an adjustment period, as it took us a while to get used to the way the other person did things. Elaine and I had some disagreements over simple household functions, such as how the toilet paper should be hung on the dispenser or which way the roll of kitchen paper towels should be facing on the towel rack. With time, these little disputes tended to work themselves out.

We found our blended family to be the most challenging issue in our marriage. She had three adult children, and I had no children, but my mother and father were still living. Sometimes in a blended family, certain family members can do things that will cause problems between the husband and wife. For example, a non-biological family member such as a stepchild or in-law might openly show dislike and continually disrespect the new husband or new wife. This can result in arguments between the couple, putting a strain on their marriage. Frequently, when conflict exists, people just don't stop and think about how their actions are affecting others. In the beginning, Elaine was the only one who stopped to consider how her actions might have harmful consequences on others in our family. So initially our blended family had arguments that turned into more than they needed to be. This caused a great deal of tension between Elaine and me, but we worked through these situations. We learned how to keep their actions from creating so much tension between us.

As a result of these disagreements, I matured and became a better person. Elaine taught me to stop and think about how my reactions to the wrongdoings of others would affect the feelings of everyone, not just the person I had an issue with. I used to get into some heated arguments with Elaine's youngest son. I learned to let some of the less serious issues slide. However, sometimes action needs to be taken, but the wrong course of action can be hurtful to those who are not involved and make things worse. There are many different ways of handling a crisis that will produce the same results without causing long-lasting resentments. For instance, if Elaine's youngest son did something that was extremely wrong, rather than getting into a heated argument with him, I would wait and discuss what he did in private with Elaine. We would decide together what course of action we would take. This kept Elaine and me in agreement, and we had way fewer arguments.

After Elaine passed away, I felt guilty about some of the really bad arguments we had, and I needed to remind myself that no one is perfect. In many cases, the roots of these arguments stemmed from the actions of others. Yet the most important thing was that we loved each other; we stayed together and worked through everything. I have to give Elaine all of the credit for this, as she was way smarter than I will ever be.

To close this chapter, I want to leave you with this thought: There is no reason to make something you regret into something you did wrong. Even if you did do some things that were wrong, your loved one probably has forgiven you. So you need to forgive yourself.

Do we Have Guilt or Regret?

Even if that person did not forgive you, you still need to forgive yourself! No one on the face of this Earth is a flawless human being; we all make mistakes. No matter what happened, the loved one you lost, this person who also loved you, would not want you living in guilt. Just learn from your mistakes. Live the rest of your life to make your loved one proud, and someday when you see that person in heaven, all will be forgiven. I hope this chapter helps you find freedom from any guilt that you may have.

There's No Place like Home

WHEN SOMEONE YOU LOVE DIES, if that person has lived in the same house with you, your feelings about your home can change. I have known people who lost a spouse and say that when they were in their house, they felt connected with the loved one who had passed. These people will usually follow up a statement like this by stating, "Nothing would ever make me leave my home until the day I die." Then there are those of us who feel just the opposite: our home becomes a place we absolutely hate.

GRIEF

If you are old enough, you might remember the classic film *The Wizard of Oz*. The movie was released August 25, 1939, starring Judy Garland. It was nominated for six Academy Awards, including Best Picture, but lost to *Gone with the Wind*. In 1956, CBS reintroduced *The Wizard of Oz*, and due to its popularity it was televised quite frequently for many years. *The Wizard of Oz* has been a source of many quotes in our popular culture. Just in case you are too young to have ever seen this movie, the main character discovers, after facing many dangers, that all she had to do to get back home was to tap her heels together while saying, "There's no place like home. There's no place like home." That is most definitely 100 percent true. I have seen that quote many times on decorative plaques at home and garden centers. If we give this some thought, our home is the place where we normally feel the safest. Our home is our sanctuary; not only does our home shelter us from the harsh elements of the weather, but it also is where we can relax and let our guard down. Most of us, after working all day, walk through the door of our home and exhale a sigh of relief. We have had a long day dealing with the stresses of our jobs and life's other obstacles. Whether we live in a mansion that has golden chandeliers or a shack with holes in the wall, our home is our refuge away from the unpleasant things we all must face in our everyday lives.

After my wife died, if I could have sold and left our home the very next day, I would have! I felt that way only after my wife died. When she was alive, the time we spent together in our home was very pleasant and I enjoyed living there. After she died, our home only triggered my grief.

Unfortunately, in 2009 the bottom had fallen out of the housing market and the economy was not good. Even houses listed way below current market value were not selling. I considered some other options such as renting out our home and moving into an apartment, or buying another house. However, after I looked over my choices, the only practical solution I had was to continue living there even though I despised every minute.

Before we bought our house, my wife and I had agreed that we wanted a place we liked, but not something so expensive that we would have to spend every penny we earned to pay the mortgage. We had looked at several houses, but none of them were right for us. We were starting to think we were not going to find a place; then we found an old house in the country.

Although the place needed a lot of work, we could visualize how nice this house could be with some improvements. There are some women who would have wanted a brand-new house, but my wife was not like that. She was not materialistic or concerned with impressing anyone. We both just wanted a home where we could be comfortable and enjoy our life together. This old country house was far from elaborate, yet we knew we were buying something that was hard to find: a place in a quiet, peaceful setting. The house was situated on a half acre with a fair amount of woods on the back of the property, which gave us privacy. Not only that, but my wife also loved nature, particularly trees and especially in the fall when the leaves change colors.

There was also a huge flower bed that ran the entire length of the sidewalk. We planted flowers during the growing season, and in the cool of the evening I would water and fertilize the flowers for her. Sometimes she would stand on the porch and supervise. The kitchen was small, but there was a glass door and a huge glass panel leading from the kitchen to the outside. My wife used to tell me that she liked this kitchen because when she was cooking, she could look out and see the lake in the distance and the lilac bush in our yard. I used to pull lilacs from that bush for her and put them in the living room on the mantle. The living room was large with a working fireplace. In the winter, we used to sit in front of a roaring fire and watch the snow fall to the ground, covering our front yard. My wife always enjoyed reading a good book in this room, especially during the winter when we were using the fireplace.

In July and August, we would come home after work and cool off by swimming in the pool. My wife used to say that she felt rich because we had a pool. I told her we were far from wealthy, as we had only an aging above-ground pool. As I think back on this now, I realize we had everything we needed. So I think being rich, in Elaine's mind, was not about our bank account, but about the joy and happiness that came from being together and swimming in the cool water under the moonlight. We used to paddle around in the pool and look up at the stars in the sky; I would often take hold of her hands and pull her around the pool.

We occasionally had family get-togethers to swim and cook out, but we also celebrated numerous happy holidays in that house. These special times shared with people we love are the things that transform a house into a home. Every time we would come in the gate or leave, one of us would comment on the country setting, the trees, the lake, or how blue the water in the pool looked. My wife would often admire her flower bed. She would smile whenever a new flower started to bloom. We had built a huge, two-level wooden deck onto the back of the house. The bottom was twelve feet wide and forty feet long, and the top was twelve feet wide and thirty feet long with French doors leading from our bedroom out onto the top deck. We were slowly fixing things up the way we wanted, and we were very happy living there.

I can remember details about the first week after my wife died, but not the order in which they happened. Although I do not know the exact day this happened, because there were several people at the house at different times that week, on one occasion my son-in-law arrived with Elaine's daughter, my stepdaughter. He came inside and told me that my stepdaughter needed a few minutes before she could come into the house. Not long after that, the side door leading into our kitchen opened, and Elaine's daughter entered. When she closed the door, I heard a loud, piercing cry coming from the kitchen. A few weeks later my stepdaughter told me that in the past, whenever she came to our house and would walk through the door, she knew her mother would be inside. She said she used to go from room to room, calling out, "Mom, where are you?" But the first time she came to the house after her mother had passed away, she cried so pitifully because she knew she would never again be able to find her mother. She went on to say that she would come to the house to see me, but that she really did not even like to look at the house because she knew her mother was not inside. I understood exactly how she felt; I also was having a lot of trouble being in the house.

The day my wife died, when I came home and walked through the door, my stomach was in knots. Consequently, this time I did not exhale a sigh of relief. The total silence in the house was disturbing. I knew my wife was not upstairs; she was no place in the house, nor would she ever be again. She was gone forever! I remember saying out loud, "It was all for nothing. This place means nothing to me anymore!" I felt very angry but also lost. This house was no longer my home. I felt as though I were in a strange place. Elaine and I had picked out this house together, but she was dead and the house would never be the same without her. I stood there in the living room, looking around and feeling an emptiness inside my soul. I saw the helium-filled balloons I had bought her for Valentine's Day, now starting to look a little tattered and leaking helium. Then I saw the seven-inch-tall cloth ghost we used to use as a paper weight, sitting on the mantle over the fireplace. This was too much for me to stand. I walked through the house, crying out loud, "This cannot be real! I must be having a bad dream!"

Yet not just the inside of the house bothered me—the outside was also a problem. Every time I walked through the gate to leave or come home, my late wife's flower bed was there, and this reminded me of her smile. Every time I walked out the door to go to the car, the swimming pool was there, and this reminded me of all those late-night swims with her. Every time I looked across the backyard, the woods were there; I would look at those trees and I could almost hear her voice saying how green the trees looked. Not only did my wife and I spend time together in and around our home, but we also followed routines, so we almost always knew each other's whereabouts.

She died in March. By April, the grass needed to be cut. As I started driving the riding mower across the lower portion of the backyard, I looked up the hill at our home, and I knew Elaine was not in the upstairs office on the computer. I realized she would not be walking out onto the top level of the deck to wave at me. I stopped the mower because I could not see to drive, as my eyes were filled with tears. It was impossible for me to function. I remember thinking, *How am I going to live in this house?*

I had to do some things to make living there mentally easier on me, because I felt like I was losing my mind. At a grief group, someone had suggested putting some of Elaine's things out of sight. Putting things away will help—that is no secret—but I felt so bad that I did not believe anything would ever help me. For several weeks I could not bring myself to touch or move her belongings. I finally was able to start putting some of her personal things away, even though doing so was difficult.

I began with belongings that were tremendously hurtful for me to see: her books. She had hundreds of them. Most were in our home office, but some were on a bookcase in the living room, and others were scattered throughout the downstairs. Reading had been an enormous part of Elaine's life—it was a part of who she was. The books were a representation of her love for reading, and seeing her books was like looking at a billboard that said *Elaine*. So every time I saw her books, they reminded me of her. The only problem with that was she was dead! I put her books in the upstairs closet where I could not see them; this produced some immediate feelings of relief. I could then look at those areas where the books used to be without being reminded of my late wife. I never wanted to forget her, but for the time being I needed to remove some of the things that instantly made me think of her. I was grieving and thinking about her enough, so I surely did not need objects in the house triggering my grief.

After I had finished with the books, I worked on putting other items away. This was a double-edged sword, because these knick-knacks, clothing, and other personal items that belonged to Elaine were very dear to her, so I had mixed feelings about removing them. I had to remind myself that I was doing this only temporarily to relieve some of my pain. After all, these things could always be put back in their original places later if I changed my mind.

For me, the next step was to rearrange the furniture, a change that can make a huge difference and is a quick, simple fix that does not cost any money. You might even want to temporarily put a colorful quilt or blanket over a chair or sofa to give the room a new look. If your deceased loved one used to sit in a certain spot, moving or donating that piece of furniture might relieve a great deal of your pain. At some point you might want to consider buying some different furniture. You do not have to replace everything unless you want to. You would be surprised at how much replacing a few pieces of furniture will help. However, the more you can change, the better off you will be. Adding an area rug can have a positive effect by making a room feel a lot different. Changing the decor in some of the rooms is ideal. What you want to do is create a new atmosphere. The purpose of making these transitions is to remove triggers that stir up the feelings of grief. So if you had shared an interest in horses and old westerns with your spouse who has passed away, do not hang pictures of cowboys riding horses on the wall!

Think of a topic that only you are interested in. Get creative! For example, reflect on your childhood or high school days. If you had a model train as a kid and still like trains, what about a room with pictures of old steam engines? I was a black belt in my youth. What were you excited about? Hot rods, motorcycles, sports, fishing? These are generally things men like. If you are a woman, you may like these things too, but maybe you also like quilting, knitting, painting, or photography. What about old movie memorabilia? Did you ever want to have a room displaying posters and memorabilia from your favorite movie? There are thousands of themes and different ways you can decorate a room.

Changing the furniture around in the house helped me to cope. But when I started adding decor to create specific themes, the end result was far more effective. I cannot stress this point enough! Designing new room themes is so powerful because you are not just rearranging the room to give it a different look, but you are also creating areas that display what you like. After you are done, when you walk in the room, you feel good, and you may even feel a sense of accomplishment in a job well done. When we are having difficulty living in our homes, any time we can walk into a room and feel good again is equivalent to a drowning man coming up for a breath of air. Changing the decor will give you safe areas in the house that will not trigger your grief. You will slowly take back your home, one room at a time.

I began doing this by moving the bedroom downstairs and putting the office where the bedroom used to be. Then I gathered up everything that had our local college football team's logo and moved all of that stuff into the home office to create a sports theme. In the living room, I then created an Asian look with an oriental rug, some plants, several pictures, and a large dragon tapestry. My last and final change was to hang my black belt on the wall with some old photos of myself (from my younger days) doing martial arts. After making all of these adjustments, I was better able to function inside the house. I would suggest that if you make changes, leave some things the same. I did leave some of my late wife's belongings in the house, but only the ones that did not affect me in a negative way. There is no specific type of item that will help you feel comfort rather than be a painful reminder of your loss. We all are individuals with our own thoughts and feelings. So, you will have to determine for yourself what to keep out and what should be packed away.

The outside was an entirely different matter, as there were limitations to what could be done. Actually, nothing could be done about some of the things that bothered me. I hired someone to mow my yard the first two years after my wife's death. That kept me from being on the mower and looking up at the house, which was a reminder that my wife was not inside. I also created a different look with the flower bed by adding a concrete dragon, some temples, and other Asian statues. I gave that flower bed a completely different look. Afterward, when I looked at the flower bed, I felt proud of what I had accomplished and not deep sorrow.

I know that sounds strange. Maybe a better way to explain this would be to say that when I looked at Elaine's flowers, I could see her smiling face in my mind's eye, which made me start to tear up. After my changes, I would focus on the bright green dragon that sat among the flowers.

Somehow my emotions mixed together so that I felt the sadness over my wife's death but also happiness about what I had created in the flower bed. As a result, I could think of my wife and feel sad but not become completely overwhelmed to the point of feeling my life was hopeless. In my sadness I even found myself feeling grateful for the time I had shared with her working on the flower bed. For the first time since her death, I felt like I was going to be okay. I think having some new things in the flower bed to focus on helped to keep the grief from engulfing me. I was able to push the grief away quickly and go on with my day. I remember walking past the flower bed and thinking that Elaine would not like the dragon but would tell me she was proud of all the hard work I had done—and I felt good about leaving her flowers in place with my new creation. When I watered them, I would think of her and miss her, sad that she was not there with me. However, the flower bed was no longer a trigger that submerged me in grief.

There was nothing that could be done about the woods, unless I wanted to chainsaw all the trees down. I could have taken the above-ground pool down. However, the only problem was that we had replaced the old pool with a new one a year before my wife died. Those pools are way more expensive than advertised! From an appraisal standpoint, they do not add any value to one's house, but I still thought this amenity might be a plus to a prospective buyer if someday I did try to sell. So I just had to deal with looking at the pool, even though I did not want to. To keep the water from turning green, I had to open the pool every summer so the water could circulate. Sometimes I had to get in the pool in order to do this. Just getting in the pool was so hard on me that I would break down in tears. This task was so painful for me that the first two summers I remember praying for God to help me get through opening and closing the pool. I still would let my late wife's kids and grandkids come to the house and swim, but that was only once in a while. After she died, I never really used the pool. Even though using the pool got easier after some years went by, swimming at home just never was the same for me without Elaine.

Although we can make some physical changes to the house, how can we change what we cannot put our hands on? I'm talking about the routines that have become so much a part of our everyday lives that we expect them to occur. Our mind knows when these activities normally occur, but we also know the person we shared these things with is gone, and that is very painful. For some people, following their old patterns is tremendously distressing. Forming new routines helps; however, our minds can be slow to adjust because in our grief we sometimes tend to emphasize our thoughts about the past.

After work, my late wife and I would often sit in the living room watching and discussing our favorite TV programs. I could no longer sit in the living room and watch TV, much less watch the same TV shows she and I had watched together. I knew that I would have to find new things to do.

Every night on the drive home after work, my mind would think about pulling in the driveway and walking into an empty house, which only made things worse for me. But something was about to happen that was going to help. One night after work, as I was walking through the house, I glanced out the glass panel door. To my surprise, I saw a large Siamese cat looking inside. I started putting food out for this cat, but after some investigation, I found out he could possibly belong to the eighty-nine-year-old lady who lived next door. I did not want to steal someone else's pet, so I went next door to discuss this matter with the elderly woman.

At first she was nervous, thinking that maybe the cat had done some damage to my car. After I told her there was no problem and that I was just looking for the owner because the cat had been coming over to my house, she looked relieved. She told me that the cat belonged to her. Yet when I started to hand the cat to her, she said, "No, he stays outside." Then she told me he had been going to other houses in the area as well as mine, because she had not put any food out in three days. It was obvious that the cat did not really belong to her but was just one of many wandering homeless cats in the area that she occasionally would feed.

I set the cat down on her concrete porch, and that big Siamese rolled over on his back and tried to nestle himself into the hard concrete as if he were lying on a soft feather bed.

I asked the elderly woman if the cat had a name. She said it was Baby. I thought to myself, *What a stupid name for this cat.* He was way too courageous to be named Baby. I had watched him walk around my yard and the surrounding areas like he was a lion surveying his kingdom. When he walked, he either moved at a leisurely pace, looking around with no fear, or stealthily prowled like he was stalking his next meal.

I had learned to appreciate cats only after I met my late wife. Before I met Elaine, I was a dog lover. I wanted to keep the cat, but the elderly woman thought the cat belonged to her, and no matter what his life had once been, he was now a free spirit. He went where he wanted to go, when he wanted to go, and he answered to no one. It would have been a shame to take this majestic cat's freedom away by restricting him to the inside of a house, at least while the weather was still warm.

So I reached down to pet the cat, and as I walked away, I said, "Well, I have to go, but if Baby comes over to my house again, I will give him some food and send him back over to you." The elderly woman thanked me. I had a mindset that she and I could just share the cat, but I knew one thing for sure: I was not going to call him Baby.

When he came over to my house the next evening, I had a talk with him. Yes, I talk to animals, and though I am not a Dr. Dolittle, cats and dogs seem to understand me. I told Baby that when he was at my house his name was going to be Simon, as that would be short for Siamese. He seemed to like the name; in fact, I could even call him and he would come to me.

After Simon came into my life, while I was driving home from work, I found myself not only thinking about my late wife and the empty house, but also wondering if Simon would show up for his evening meal.

Some nights he was there, and other nights he was not. I never knew if Simon would be waiting on the porch or if he would show

GRIEF

up a half hour after I was home. On nights the cat did not show up, I got worried that something had happened to him.

Now you may be thinking that I have lost my mind by talking about some stray cat. But because Simon did not have a set schedule, I had something to concentrate on while I was driving home. When I pulled into the driveway I would be thinking, *Is Simon on the porch or will he be stopping by later?* This was a lot better than thinking about walking into an empty house. The cat did not totally take my mind off of my loss, but I now had a new evening routine. It may have been something as simple as feeding a stray cat. But the main point is that my mind was at least starting to associate coming back to the house with something new.

I am currently still living in my house several years after her death. I cannot tell you if you should leave your home or stay there. Neither is right or wrong—you must do what feels best for you. What I do know is that I am now glad I stayed and dealt with my grief. The house will never be the same without Elaine, but I do feel comfortable living there, and this house has become my home once again. Someday, if I do leave, I will do so because I want to, not because the memories and grief are forcing me to.

What Should I Do with Belongings?

THE PERSONAL PROPERTY that someone owns can be a good indication of what type of person he or she is. Yet people can be complicated, so it is best never to assume that an individual fits into only one category. People can make assumptions about who we are without truly knowing us. There is a lot more to a person than just an occupation, education, physical appearance, or background. These things might be a part of us, but by no means do they encapsulate who we are. I feel that people's imperfections, strengths, weaknesses, and moral values are the essence of who they truly are. All of us have accomplished goals and have been through personal struggles that only we, or the people closest to us, know about. So there is much more to an individual than what we might perceive based only on our surface impressions.

People's interests may be a part of them, but it is what they are passionate about that becomes an essential part of their internal mind, soul, and nature, which makes them unique.

Whether a person aspires to someday become a great artist or to paint only as a hobby, the completion of a painting brings that person great joy. The people who love them see this joy and know how important creating art is to their loved one.

If you and I stood in the studio of an artist who has passed away, we might only see paint brushes, easels, and blank canvases as we looked around the room. To us, the paint brushes are nothing more than tools used to paint. However, someone who is grieving the death of this artist might look at those same paint brushes and recall many instances of seeing the beloved artist using them. We could look at one of the paintings this artist had finished and admire the detail or brilliant colors. Yet to someone who is grieving, this same painting might bring deep feelings of comfort

What Should I Do with Belongings?

or overwhelming sorrow. These feelings happen not only because the painting represents something that was of great significance to the person lost, but also because there are special memories associated with the painting, such as the joy that the loved one felt after completing this piece of art. There might even be a memory of the artist's smiling face and a conversation that took place about this particular painting. When someone we love is no longer here, recalling these things can sometimes be tremendously hurtful because we know we will never again be able to share these experiences.

Think about how many of us have that family member who is a fan of a sports team. This person watches the games and wears hats, shirts, and jackets with the team's logo. This person might even have a jersey and some autographed items, and he or she maybe even attends the games. We hear this family member bragging about the team after a win, boasting about an awesome play that won the game. Of course, this person is sad when the team is defeated and will sometimes even get angry if someone is talking badly about the team. When this family member passes away, these personal items that are associated with the team are left behind. These things are reminders of something this person enjoyed that was a significant part of his or her life.

I have heard people in grief groups say that they did not know what to do with the personal property of their deceased loved ones. Although most people knew exactly what to do with some of their loved one's belongings, there always seemed to be some items that were more difficult to know what to do with. Letting go of personal property that used to belong to someone you loved who has passed away can be emotionally painful. Sometimes it's keeping those belongings that can be painful, but keeping them can also be comforting.

Grief

I think that the more sentimental a person is, the more difficult it can be to make these kinds of decisions, especially when one is grieving. In reality, we never have to do anything with the personal belongings of our loved ones, unless there are some legal or financial responsibilities that require immediate action. If you tend to be an emotional person, the question is not so much what to do with particular items, but what can be done with them that will allow you to feel peace in your heart and mind. What matters the most is that you can live with your choices—not only today, but also years from now.

A perfect example of this is a story about a high school friend of mine. I graduated from high school in the mid-1980s; we were a more hands-on generation. Most young guys were talking about getting a sharp car, truck, or motorcycle. I had a buddy who was really into cars—actually cars were his hobby. My friend had a nice 1969 Camaro that he was restoring. He personally rebuilt the motor and added a few extras to increase the horsepower. Although he loved his Camaro, that car was just his everyday mode of transportation.

His true pride and joy was his classic 1955 Chevy. The car was bright yellow—you could see it on the road from a mile away. The motor roared with power when he accelerated. Everyone knew who owned the yellow '55 Chevy; after all, even in the 1980s, one seldom saw a classic car like this driving down the road. My friend was always working on his cars. His dream was to someday completely restore his '55 Chevy and enter it into car shows.

But my buddy never got to enter his yellow '55 Chevy into any car show himself. He died on a lonely country road when his Camaro exploded into flames, crashing into a large boulder at the onset of the first of two hairpin curves. He left behind not only his Chevy, but also a fiancée and an unborn child.

After his death, his father did a full restoration of the Chevy, making his son's dream become a reality. The car received a new engine with all the high-performance racing extras his son had talked about getting for the car but did not have the funds for. The car was reconditioned and built just the way his son had planned to do someday. When the car was finished, it was entered in several car shows in the memory of the young man who had passed away in that terrible car crash.

After one year of showing the car, on the anniversary on his son's death, his father took the car to a junkyard and put his son's dream machine in a car crusher. This beautiful 1955 Chevy, which had thousands of dollars invested in its restoration and hundreds of hours of hard work, was reduced to a block of metal by the powerful force of the car crusher in a matter of minutes.

I can only speculate what this man thought. Perhaps he felt that since his son had left this world, so should the car. Restoring the vehicle was therapeutic for this father; he would often talk about his son while working on the car. But the destruction of his son's car seemed to be something he needed to do before moving on with his own life. He did not want to keep the car or loan it to a car museum. Selling was not an option because it just did not seem right for anyone to drive his son's '55 Chevy. After the car was crushed, my buddy's father almost seemed relieved. He had to put the pain of his son's death behind him, and crushing the car was a step toward this.

I do not think my friend's father ever regretted his decision to crush the car. He did not act impulsively out of grief, as he took plenty of time to think about what he wanted to do with the vehicle. I have also known people who have done exactly the opposite by keeping a classic car that belonged to someone who had passed and taking it for an occasional drive. They also made plans to restore the vehicle and someday pass it down to another family member.

I have given you two examples of people who have done completely different things with cars that formerly belonged to a now-deceased loved one. Although each family handled their cars in separate ways, both cases are acceptable. However, I feel it is a mistake when one disposes of a loved one's belongings hastily because of overwhelming grief or anger. This can result in discarding something that one later wishes had been kept. The opposite side of this is when one becomes so emotional as to attach sentimental value to items that have none. This can make it difficult for a person to let go of anything. After my wife's death, in the beginning I felt terrible about discarding some small items that were in a junk drawer. After time went by, I became less emotional and was able to realize that there was no reason for me to feel bad about throwing away stuff that my wife herself would have thrown away if she were alive.

Nevertheless, I still had conflicting feelings about what to do with my late wife's belongings. A lot of her possessions were things I was never going to use or had no interest in. However, getting rid of her stuff just felt wrong. I had some special memories of times I had shared with her that were attached to certain items, such as a small ghost that was a Halloween decoration named "Boo." I bought

What Should I Do with Belongings?

this ghost for my wife during the first October of our marriage. Then there was the stuffed bear I gave her before we even started dating. Both of these items had a lot of sentimental value. I knew I would never part with these objects, but seeing them caused me pain. Fortunately, I was able to realize that I needed to keep certain items that were special even though they triggered my grief.

The question of what to do with our loved one's belongings is not a hard question. The hard question is: *What am I going to do with the belongings that will allow me to feel like I have made the right decision and to feel peace in my heart?* Ultimately, we have only five different options:

1. We keep some.
2. We give some to other family members.
3. We donate some to charity.
4. We sell some.
5. We throw some away.

Going through this process of deciding what to do with stuff can be emotionally painful. Sometimes the best way to get through this is in stages—in intervals of days, weeks, and even months. This gives you a break and allows time to think about the choices you are making.

I found that asking myself whether my wife would approve of my decisions was extremely helpful. Because she was deceased, I obviously could not have a real conversation with her, but there was a way to get her input without actually talking to her in person. Now, you may not believe this is possible, so let me ask you this question: Have you ever been around a family member when something happened, and you knew what that person's reaction would be, even before he or she said or did anything? You may have even said, "I knew you were going to say that," or, "I knew you were going to do that."

GRIEF

This shows that you really know a person. My wife and I could predict how each other would react to different situations most of the time. I will not claim to have been able to read her mind, but I did know how she felt and what she was thinking about many things. Therefore, I could absolutely have a make-believe conversation with her about the decisions I was making, which helped me tremendously.

Because Elaine did not have a will, I had to rely on what she had told me and on my own instincts. My late wife was passionate about reading. Most of her books were murder mysteries or trilogies such as the Harry Potter books or *The Lord of the Rings*. She did tell me that if anything ever happened to her, I should give her book collection to her daughter and daughter-in-law, as both girls liked to read. She wanted me to give half of her books to each girl and tell them that after they both had read one of her books, they should swap with each other. Elaine told me that she knew her death would be hard on everyone. Trading the books with each other would not only give both girls an opportunity to enjoy reading all of the books, but it would also ensure that they kept in contact with each other. This would give them the chance to comfort each other in this difficult time. As a result, Elaine's daughter told me that when she was reading her mother's books, every time she turned a page, she felt like her mother was reading with her. She told me that because her mom's hands had also touched every page, she felt like her mother was with her in spirit. I was satisfied that something that had mattered so much to my late wife was now in the care of her children.

Elaine's books had an entirely opposite effect on me. Seeing them caused me psychological and physical pain. I would feel a vast emptiness inside, and my stomach would be in knots. Seeing her books only reminded me that she was gone, so I did not want to

What Should I Do with Belongings?

see them. The books had been moved out of the main living areas of my home, but getting them completely out of the house was a huge relief. Something that had been an essential part of my late wife's life brought her daughter comfort but caused me tremendous pain. Just like the paint brushes and paintings the deceased artist left behind, my late wife's books affected each person in different ways.

If we were not extremely close to the person who passed, seeing their belongings will usually not cause us much pain. Most likely we will be affected in a neutral way. If we did have a close relationship with the person who passed away, what we are thinking when we see specific items can prompt a wide range of emotions. My stepdaughter and I both loved my late wife, yet Elaine's books affected us so differently. When I looked at the books, I would think about all the times I saw my wife sitting in our living room reading. I knew she was gone forever, and I would never see her reading there again. Although my stepdaughter had seen her mom read, she had not lived with her mother in several years. I think this is why the books did not affect her in a negative way.

We can feel comforted by having something that belonged to the person who has passed away, especially if having that item allows us to have happy thoughts or makes us feel like we have a small part of that person with us in spirit. Although many of my late wife's belongings triggered my grief, there were also items that helped me feel comfort.

I did precisely what I thought my late wife would have wanted me to do with almost everything she left behind. However, I did make one decision based on what I thought was right regarding her two sewing machines. The obvious choice would have been to give one of the machines to Elaine's daughter and the other to her daughter-in-law. I was sure my late wife probably would have wanted me to do this. The problem was that neither of the two girls knew how to use a sewing machine, nor had they expressed any interest in sewing. I wanted to give her sewing machines to someone who was interested in sewing. The only solution I could come up with was to donate the sewing machines to the secondhand store in the hope that a thrifty shopper might buy them and put them to good use.

When I arrived at a particular secondhand store, for some reason I felt it was not the right place for Elaine's sewing machines. I became somewhat emotional and ended up sitting in the parking lot, unable to enter and donate the sewing machines. I thought about it over the next two weeks, but I could not come up with any options that felt right. Then, just by coincidence, I found out about a church that was looking for sewing machines. I was not sure if I would donate Elaine's sewing machines there, but it was worth looking into.

When I got to the church, I learned that some members of the congregation used sewing machines to make very small quilts. These quilts were then given to people in wheelchairs so that they could cover their legs if they got chilled. My late wife had always wanted to learn how to make quilts as a hobby. She had read some books but never actually attempted to make a quilt.

The woman in charge asked me if I would like to see a quilt that her group of volunteers had made. As we walked through the church,

What Should I Do with Belongings?

she said, "The quilt I am going to show you is not a wheelchair quilt but one that the ladies made for our church." When we got to a large room in the middle of the church, my guide proudly pointed to a wall where the huge quilt hung. It was made out of many pieces of brightly colored fabric with an image of an angel sewn in the center. As I stood there admiring the beautiful quilt, I fought to hold back my tears. My wife's maiden name was Elaine Marie Angel. I left Elaine's sewing machines at that church. I knew I had found the place where they belonged. Elaine never got a chance to make one quilt with her sewing machines, but now these machines would be making many quilts. In my heart I felt totally at peace with my decision, and I knew Elaine would approve.

Although we may keep and cherish some special things that belonged to our lost loved one, finding new places for some of the other belongings is part of putting the past behind us. It helps to remember that the most precious things our loved one left behind for us are the memories we have of the many special times we shared together.

If you have been struggling with what to do with your lost loved one's belongings, hopefully this chapter has helped and given you a fresh perspective. If you take your time, think rationally, and follow your heart, you will make the right decisions.

What Is Journaling and Can It Help Me?

WHAT IS JOURNALING, and does it help? According to english.stackexchange.com, "A personal journal is a record of significant experiences. It is much more personal than a diary. It contains feelings, emotions, problems, and self-assurances, and it can be used to evaluate one's life. For a journal, one does not just record one's experiences, but also thoughts, feelings, and reflections."

People can journal in many different ways. This chapter is

about a form of journaling that I found to be extremely helpful. When my wife died, my mind was flooded with memories of the times we shared with each other. I was recalling my entire life with her in detail. I was grieving so badly that I felt like I was going to lose my mind. So I started journaling to record my thoughts; many people do this as therapy. Although it began as therapy, for me it evolved into much more. I was not just journaling about my present feelings over my loss, but I was recording the many memories of the special times I had shared with my late wife. This eventually resulted in something exceptional that honored my wife's memory, in addition to something that was instrumental in my grief recovery.

I feel this is one of the most important chapters in this book. I truly believe that if I had not started journaling, mentally I would not be in as good of a place as I am now. You should consider journaling if you have recently lost a loved one and your mind is swamped with memories that are affecting you in a negative way.

When thinking about journaling, some people may feel uncertain about what to write or how to start. You can begin any way you want and write whatever you want! A journal is very personal; you do not have to reveal what you are writing to anyone. If you happen to make some mistakes, no big deal! The purpose of journaling is to see if the process of writing will help you with your grief. So do not let the thought of writing intimidate you in any way. Even if you think putting things down on paper is not going to help, you may find the results surprising. I want to share my method with you because I found it to be a very powerful tool in my grief recovery.

If my way of journaling is going to help you, after your first attempt you should feel a little better. However, journaling is a process that one reaps the benefits of a little bit at a time. For example, an

What Is Journaling and Can It Help Me?

athlete will do strenuous exercises for several weeks or months to achieve top physical condition, going through physical pain to reach the maximum potential for competing. Someone who is grieving and writing about the lost loved one will be going through a great deal of emotional pain. This is very hard, and you have to find inner strength to be able to endure it. Nevertheless, I found that the pain I went through while journaling was well worth the end results.

When I made my decision to begin journaling, I knew I was going to write about the memories that randomly kept popping into my mind. However, instead of just the initial memories that came to me, I wanted to include details about the circumstances surrounding those memories. For instance, if I started thinking about a conversation we had while on vacation, I would write about everything that was happening during that time. I composed these memories into short stories. It almost felt like I had traveled back in time and was reliving the past. I could recall every small detail, right down to what she was wearing. I could even remember a breeze blowing inland from the ocean or what the air smelled like on a particular summer night as we sat outside talking and listening to the crickets chirp.

The first time I journaled, I had no idea it would affect me so intensely. I had to stop and regain my composure several times because my eyes would begin to fill with tears. I thought reliving these memories was painful, but when I started to read my stories back to myself out loud, I found out what real pain was. I began to get upset and had to stop reading. I tried a second and third time without any success. I tried one last time to read out loud what I had written. That time I was able to read completely from the beginning to the end without stopping. When my eyes filled with tears, I would wipe them away so I could see the words on the page again. When I got to parts that made me start to cry, I kept reading even though my voice was trembling and I felt like I was dying inside. When I was finished, the page was wet from my tears, and my hands were shaking. This experience caused me extreme anguish.

But do you know what happened the next morning? Something was very different when I woke up. My stomach did not seem to feel like it was in knots! I remember lying in bed, waiting to see what was going to happen. Then I sat up in bed and put my feet on the floor. Although I still felt a little anxious, I could tell a huge difference. I was finally feeling some relief from my nervousness.

I knew that journaling had helped me, so from that point on, I started writing every night. Writing never really got easy for me. I can say without any exaggeration that if I had been able to save my tears, they would have filled up a fifty-gallon barrel. This is the exact reason that journaling helped me: my deep sorrow and pain over my wife's death was leaving my body one teardrop at a time. Journaling may not have this kind of impact on you or affect you with this degree of intensity, but journaling can help you in various ways.

Even though writing helped me to get a lot of my sadness out, what actually helped me the most was forcing myself to read back over what I had written and *read it out loud* until I could do so without being upset. Reading out loud made journaling a thousand times more effective for me. Yet one might think that because I was getting so upset, I was only hurting myself. I was causing myself a lot of pain, yes, but I was also helping myself get rid of my sorrow. I have heard people say grief only gets easier with time. However, I do not believe it is merely the passing of time, but what is taking place during that time—things like accepting the loss, starting to adjust to life being different, and just getting the sadness out. My method of journaling definitely helped me to not keep my sadness bottled up, and this allowed me to start feeling better.

For me, using the computer was a much better way to journal than pen and paper. After I completed a story, I would print out a hard copy to read back to myself. If you have a computer, I highly recommend that you try this. The physical act of tapping the keys can give you the opportunity to relieve some built-up anxiety. There was something about striking the keys rather than writing with a pen that just seemed to feel right to me. Using the computer also allowed me to backspace and make changes if I wanted to.

Everyone is different, so if you want to use pen and paper, that is perfectly fine. I have heard people say that when they used a pen, they felt like their thoughts and feelings were almost flowing out of their body and onto the paper. Remember that the reason you are journaling is to release your emotions, so choose the best method for you.

I had been journaling for only a few weeks when I became aware that there were many details in the stories that only my late wife and I knew about, and I was now the only one who could tell them. I did not want these memories to die with me, so I decided to make a memory book for the family (especially the grandchildren). When Elaine passed away, some of her grandchildren were toddlers, while others were not around us a lot because of separation or divorce. I wanted each of them to have insight into who she was and how we lived our lives.

Most people will make a memory book containing photos of the person who has passed away, as a picture is worth a thousand words. I personally love photos as a way to visually record and save special times in our lives. But they do not tell the whole story! For example, if you were looking at a photo of your great-grandpa standing on top of a mountain, you would know he had hiked or climbed his way to the top. But what happened from the bottom of the mountain to the top of the mountain? Maybe nothing. Then again, he may have encountered a grizzly bear! You would have no idea simply by looking at a photo of him standing on the top of the mountain, nor would you know if he was excited or in fear for his life when he first laid eyes on that bear. For this reason, I decided that the memory book I was going to make to honor my late wife would contain not only photos of her, but also the stories I had been composing while I was journaling. I hoped that these stores would be cherished by the family members who had personally known Elaine, and also that they would be passed down to future generations. I knew that if my wife had still been alive, she would have been thrilled at this concept.

When I made the decision to put the stories that I had been writing into her memory book, things drastically changed, as my journaling now had a dual purpose. Not only was my journaling helping me move forward with my recovery from grief, but it was also one last thing I would be able to do for Elaine. I could give her the gift of keeping her memory alive in the hearts and minds of her grandchildren. This became my number one priority, and at the time, was absolutely the only thing that mattered to me.

Because I planned on sharing these memories with the family, what I was writing needed to be understandable by people other than myself. I suffer from dyslexia, so writing is much harder for me than for most people. I would often begin writing at eight o'clock on a Saturday morning and still be writing at eight o'clock that evening. The end result would be several pieces of paper crumpled up on the floor, with only one or two pages done. Unfortunately, what I did manage to finish was unusable because of several mistakes in my spelling and punctuation, which completely distorted what I was trying to say. I knew exactly what I wanted to write, but I had undertaken something that was extremely difficult for me. I became very disgusted—I had spent endless hours writing but had nothing that could be used in the memory book. After six months had passed, I felt like some of the family members had started to believe that Elaine's memory book was just wishful thinking that would never become reality.

After ten months had passed, I felt like giving up, but I couldn't because I would be letting my wife down. Fortunately, I finally found someone who was willing to correct my punctuation and spelling mistakes. This enabled me to make progress, as my stories could then be understood and used in the memory book.

Even though I had been working on overcoming my grief and trying to go on with my life, I still had days when I thought I could no longer stand the pain of my loss. I would tell myself that no matter how bad I felt, I had to finish Elaine's memory book. Working on other aspects of her book gave me a break from the difficult and emotionally painful process of writing. For instance, I had to be inventive with how to place the personal photos in the book. I cut a border out of blue paper to glue on the top and bottom of each page, since blue was one of Elaine's favorite colors. I also searched online for free images to place on the pages of each story, much the way people do for scrapbooks. I actually enjoyed using my creativity to design the layout, and the memory book was turning out much better than I had anticipated.

Grief

Most people who knew I was working on this project really had no specific idea about what I was doing. They just thought I was making a photo album and writing a few memories about my late wife. I am certain that the only person who truly understood the depth of what I hoped to accomplish was my grief counselor, with whom I had shared some of my stories. Also, some of the people in my grief group were very supportive of what I was doing. However, I was astonished at how many funny looks and negative comments I received from some so-called friends. They just thought I was crazy—what I was doing was taking too long, and no one would put that amount of time or work into such a project.

I feel that in life we ultimately have to do what we know is right. My wife was a good woman, and she deserved nothing less than my full effort and dedication. That is exactly what I gave. When the book was done, I wanted to show it to Elaine, but sadly that was not possible. So I went to her grave, the place where I felt the closest to her. I sat on the ground facing her gravestone and read every page out loud to her. That was my way of giving her a copy of her book.

I finished Elaine's memory book in April 2011. She had passed away in March 2009, so this project took me a little over two years to complete. After I finished the initial book, I made eighteen copies. Each memory book contained 112 pages of written memories and photos. Although I had worked very hard on this, I was having second thoughts about distributing the copies to the family. I did not know how they would react. I wondered if the grandchildren would really care about any of the things I had written. All of them were exceptionally good kids, but young children and teens can be so wrapped up in their own world. In spite of my apprehension, I made plans to meet with the family.

What Is Journaling and Can It Help Me?

I drove one hour to see three of Elaine's grandsons who were now living with Elaine's daughter's ex-husband. Because all three of them were living in the same household, and the two older boys were not close to Elaine, I only made one book for all three to share. I told the boys they could make additional copies if they chose to do so. Any thoughts I had as to whether or not I should have given copies to the family soon evaporated as the three brothers looked eagerly through the book. The oldest boy began to read out loud from the book so his two brothers could listen. They all seemed to be interested and began talking to each other about their grandmother Elaine. Soon the oldest grandson, who was doing the reading, saw a photo and story about our cat. He asked me if it was okay for him to read that story to everyone. I told him, "Sure."

He began reading, but when he got to the part that said Elaine was a cat lover, he stopped reading for a few seconds and appeared to be thinking. He and his brothers were amazed that while on vacation, Elaine had carried a piece of fish all the way from Alabama back home to Ohio for her cat. Then he looked at me and asked, "She liked cats?"

I replied, "Yes, she loved cats!" He then told me that he also loved cats. This thirteen-year-old boy continued to read, but I could see he was reading with a much stronger interest. All three boys were smiling and enjoying the story about their grandmother's cat. When he was done reading, all three sat in silence, and they looked very sad. Then one of them asked me how long their grandmother had owned this cat before she died. I told them it was only two years, but she spent a lot of time with the cat because the cat followed her everywhere she went. I let them know I was now taking good care of the cat, and the look of sadness on their faces seemed to leave. Then

Grief

all three boys became even more interested in the memory book. They thumbed through the pages, looking at the photos and asking me all kinds of questions. Most of the answers to their questions were in the stories that accompanied the photos. I left them that day knowing that even though Elaine was in heaven, Elaine was also there with them in the memory book.

The next day I went back to Elaine's grave to meet with Elaine's siblings, in-laws, adult children, and some more of the grandchildren. Each person to whom I gave a copy of the memory book thanked me. Some of them put the books in their cars without looking inside, and others thumbed through, glancing at the contents. I think they were surprised that what I had given them was so detailed.

Now, almost ten years after her death, I have spoken with Elaine's oldest son's daughter and son about the memory book. Both of them have kept the book I gave them. The girl, now fourteen, told me that if she ever has children, she will read the book about her grandmother to them. The boy, now twenty-one, told me there are a lot of happy memories in the book and he plans to always keep it. He went on to say that he plans on sharing these memories with his girlfriend if they someday get married. I am sure that if my late wife could have heard him say this, she would be smiling.

I would not have journaled as much or as long if my journaling had not had a dual purpose. But I am glad I did because I am 100 percent sure it helped me to reach the level of peace and acceptance of Elaine's death that I have today. You, too, might consider making a memory book for your lost loved one. It does not have to be 112 pages, and you do not have to work on it for two years. Nor do you have to give copies to family members unless you want to. Just think about making a small memory book, even one that contains five or ten special memories. Remember to do your writing at night before you go to sleep, and then read what you have written back to yourself out loud.

Hopefully this chapter has inspired you to try some form of journaling. Whether you decide to make a memory book or try another form of journaling, I hope you have favorable results.

May you wake up with less pain in your heart and relief in your soul!

Why Can't I Take off My Wedding Ring?

HAVE YOU EVER THOUGHT about why the wedding ring is worn on the fourth finger on the left hand? The tradition stems from ancient times when the Romans believed that a vein in the ring finger ran straight to the heart.

When do I stop wearing my wedding ring? is a question a lot of people have. After the death of a spouse, some of us struggle a great deal with taking off our wedding rings. There is no right or wrong in this; what matters is what feels right to you in your heart. The ring tells people you are married, so unless you want to start dating, it really does not matter in your everyday life if you are still wearing your ring. However, continuing to wear your ring might mean you are still not able to accept what has happened, and that is fine because we are all different. Never let anyone pressure you into taking off your wedding band. The decision to put the ring on was yours, so you should be the one who decides when the time is right to take off your ring.

After my wife died, I wore my ring for a long time. Removing my wedding band was something I just could not bring myself to do, but before I get into my logic and feelings on this subject, I want to share some examples that show just how strong the emotions associated with a wedding ring can be. We all have special memories that may deeply affect our ability to stop wearing our wedding rings.

When my cousin got married, I was unable to attend because at that time I was still grieving the loss of my wife very intensely. I knew my presence at such an event would only stir up a lot of memories, causing me to feel even more pain than what I was already experiencing.

On my cousin's wedding day, he did something that I regret not being able to witness in person. When the preacher asked for the rings, my cousin pulled a box out of his pocket for his bride and everyone else to see. When he opened this box, he surprised everyone with a toy ring that had a gigantic plastic diamond; there was a light inside the diamond that flashed on and off. Unfortunately, the light malfunctioned; nevertheless, everyone laughed—including his bride. After the laughter stopped, the real ring came out and his fiancée became his wife.

Why Can't I Take off My Wedding Ring?

When I heard about this, I thought about how amazing this gesture was. He took a moment that was joyful, but also tense, and he did something to relieve some of the tension, putting his soon-to-be wife at ease. What he did took a lot of guts, but he was willing to do something unconventional to help his future wife relax, and he did not care about what anyone else thought. It was a good way for him and his bride to start their life together. As they both were very young, I do not know whether or not they gave this much thought, but they will always share the memory of three wedding rings: the two they wear and that big plastic toy ring with the flashing diamond. I am sure that if the toy ring could have spoken, everyone would have heard: "This marriage will last a lifetime!"

Our society puts a lot of importance on wedding rings. When I decided to propose to my future wife, I wanted to surprise her with a nice ring, but I also wanted to be practical as I knew we would have many upcoming expenses. I looked around in different jewelry stores to compare prices and also talked with some female coworkers about their wedding rings. I did not want them to think I was being nosy or suspect that I was going to propose to Elaine, so I would start the conversation by saying, "That is a nice ring. Is that your wedding ring?" Of course, my coworker would say yes and usually hold out her hand so I could get a closer look. Then I would say, "Wow! That is a sharp ring! The diamond is really shiny!" That is all I had to say to get them to start talking about their rings. This opened the door for me to sneak in a question or two about the carat, cut, or clarity of the diamond. Their responses would vary depending on how much they actually knew. I noticed that all of them seemed to be very happy and proud of their wedding rings. But was this joy coming from just having a beautiful ring, or from the memories associated with that ring and what the ring stood for?

After I did some more research and visited several other jewelry stores, I finally found a ring I thought Elaine would like. The ring included a high-quality center stone and several other smaller diamonds. While I was writing out a check to pay for the ring, the salesman said, "Do not worry. If she says no, you can return this ring for a full refund."

We both laughed, as he said this in a joking manner, but on my drive home I started thinking, *What if she does say no?* I had planned on coming up with a special way to propose to Elaine, and I heard a great method one evening while I was listening to the radio. A woman called in to request a love song. She said her boyfriend had just proposed to her by giving her a block of ice shaped like a heart. He asked her to place the heart under a faucet and turn on the hot water. As the hot water melted the heart, a waterproof container was uncovered. Inside the container was a ring with a note that said, "Now that you have melted my heart, will you marry me?" I planned on doing this with Elaine, but I was still trying to think of a unique place where we could melt the ice. Because of what the salesman had said about Elaine possibly saying no, I was on edge and wanted to get the proposal over with. The best way to do this was to scrap my big plan and simply go to Elaine's house and ask her to marry me. That is exactly what I did!

I used to be quite amused when a guy in a movie or TV show wanted to ask a woman to marry him but could not find the right words. *Really, what's the big deal?* I thought. I figured you just said, "Will you marry me?" Well, I got a real life lesson when I tried to ask Elaine to marry me. I could not speak, not at all—the words would not come out! Elaine thought something was wrong and kept saying, "What is wrong? Just tell me." After what seemed like an eternity, I eventually was able to ask her to marry me. She said yes! Elaine was very excited, and the first thing she did was show her daughter the engagement ring. I was happy too, but also relieved to have the proposal over with. Next, Elaine and I went together to pick out my ring; I wanted a plain gold band. While we were looking at rings for men, we saw one that had some small diamonds below the surface. Elaine wanted me to get that ring because it matched hers. So I did!

We had been married for about two months when Elaine lost the center diamond out of her ring. She had bumped the top of her ring, causing the diamond and the six prongs that held it to completely shear off. Initially she did not tell me; she kept her ring hand hidden so I would not notice. We both worked at a prison, so Elaine asked several correctional officers to look in areas where she had been. But her diamond was nowhere to be found. When she finally told me, she thought I would be angry with her. She even said, "Please do not be mad." I could see she was upset, so I told her that this was just one of those unfortunate things that happen, and that I was not blaming her or angry with her in any way. I think she felt a little better, but she was still upset and even started to cry. I wanted to make her feel better, so I told her we could get another diamond to replace the original stone. What I did not tell her was that her diamond had cost $2,500, and we did not have the insurance to pay for a replacement.

What mattered the most to Elaine was not the money but the fact that she had lost the original diamond. She even said, sobbing, "I want the diamond you gave me on our wedding day! Nothing can replace that diamond!"

Grief

A few days later, Elaine walked out of our bathroom in bare feet with some great news. She had stepped on something hard, and it turned out to be her lost diamond. I will never forget how happy she looked when she showed me. After that, her friends at work and I would joke with her about losing her diamond. We would call her on the telephone and tell her we saw an inmate walk by with a big diamond earring, then ask if she still had the diamond in her wedding ring. Elaine wore her wedding ring twenty-four seven; she never took it off, and she never lost the diamond again. I did the same—my ring never came off my finger the entire time I was married.

I have shared these memories with you because even though wedding rings can cost anywhere from one hundred dollars to tens of thousands of dollars, in reality, they are nothing more than pieces of metal with polished rocks. Their monetary value is nothing in comparison to their emotional value; the memories associated with these rings are priceless. When a man asks a woman to marry him and she replies "Yes," this is a very emotional moment filled with overwhelming feelings of nervousness, fear, surprise, joy, and the most powerful emotion of all—love. This changes both of their lives forever! Usually, during the moment of the proposal, the engagement ring is given to the woman. In some cases, the couple go together and pick out their rings. These are memories that both people will have for the rest of their lives. When you wear a wedding ring, you tell the world that someone loves you and that you also love that person. The rings are such a vital part of these memories. This is why some people struggle with taking the ring off.

I have seen people who are able to stop wearing their wedding rings without too much difficulty. Yet there are others, like me, who

Why Can't I Take off My Wedding Ring?

find this to be heartbreaking. Taking my ring off was very emotionally painful. I tried several times to remove my wedding ring, but I could not. I felt like something was terribly wrong, and there was—my wife was dead! I was fearful of being disconnected from her forever. I was not willing to accept that she was gone.

I would go to Elaine's grave site, the place where I felt the most connected to her, and talk to her as if she were alive. I would share what was going on with the children and grandchildren, and I would talk to her about what was troubling me or what had happened that was good. I would also kneel and cry, sharing my deepest sorrow and grief with her.

The first time I became extremely emotional, something strange occurred. I wondered if she could hear me, and I was thinking, *If only there were a phone line to heaven, everything would be okay—then I could go on without her.* As I knelt in tears, I felt a faint breeze, which suddenly became stronger and stronger until the flowers moved on her grave. It was like something straight out of a movie. I reached out to touch the flowers, pinching one of them between my thumb and forefinger, and told her how much I loved her. Every time I went to her grave after this happened, I would look at the flowers to check if they were moving, and they always were. At first I thought this was a coincidence, or maybe that I was just losing my mind. But then I realized that if I went to the grave site when I was very troubled and feeling like my life was totally hopeless, when I would start talking, the breeze would become stronger. Often as I became increasingly upset, the breeze would become even stronger, and the flowers would bend even more vigorously. If I was at her grave on an eighty-nine-degree day in July, there would still be a faint breeze, even one so weak that one petal on one flower would move.

GRIEF

This happened every time I visited the grave. I had become convinced that Elaine's grave site was our doorway to heaven, a place in the universe where I could open the door and talk to her. I felt like this was my phone line to heaven. Although she could not talk to me, she let me know she heard me when those flowers moved. A lot of people will say this is crazy, or maybe just not believe me, but I do not really care what anyone else thinks about this. What matters to me is that I truly believe my wife can hear me, and her spirit lets me know when the wind makes the flowers move. I am not an overly religious person, but I could not come up with any scientific reason for that breeze moving those flowers every time I was there. What I do know, is that somehow I had been able to communicate with Elaine at her grave because of the love we had for each other.

After all the memories I have shared with you about wedding rings, I can safely say that a wedding ring is a symbol of the love two people have for each other. I feared that if I removed my ring, those flowers might stop moving and my doorway to heaven would be closed forever. I am sure this was an obstacle that was uniquely my own. However, it is important for you to read my experience because you may also have some unique obstacles that are preventing you from removing your wedding ring. That is normal and perfectly acceptable; we all have to deal with and work through issues in our own way.

When my wife died, I could not even think straight, much less begin to reflect on what taking off my ring represented. Some people in the grief group I attended stopped wearing their wedding rings seemingly without issue. People in my family were pressuring me to do the same. But I was not ready! There was no way I could complete such a heart-wrenching task. Taking off my wedding band

Why Can't I Take off My Wedding Ring?

would have been a step closer to overcoming the grief that I had become imprisoned by; however, I could not find the strength to move forward. Continuing to wear my ring was hindering me from getting to an emotional place where I could completely accept what had happened. At times I found myself feeling like I was living a lie, but I also felt guilt at the mere thought of taking off my wedding ring. I kept telling myself that I would wake up one morning and the thought of shedding my ring would feel acceptable, but that day never seemed to come.

I finally had to make a conscious decision to take that painful next step. I set a date on which I would force myself to remove my ring. Every time I tried, I would immediately notice a sensation of emptiness on my finger. When I started to slide off my ring, I instantly felt my finger breathe as the air hit the skin that had been restricted for so long under the smooth gold band. This was a double-edged sword—the removal of the ring felt soothing to my tightly bound finger, yet the physical sensation was an instant realization that something was not right, and not just on my finger, but in my life as well. With each attempt, I failed. I pushed the removal date back another month or two, only to fail again and push the date back even further into the future.

I had to resolve four issues within myself or I would never be able to take off my wedding ring. First, even though taking off the ring was extremely painful, I had to know and accept in my heart that nothing was going to change. She was gone. Holding on to the pain and wanting to change what was unchangeable were two things keeping me from being able to symbolically disconnect myself from her.

Second, I had to stop feeling guilty about taking off my wedding ring. Putting my wedding ring on showed that I loved her and was committed to her. A wedding ring is a symbol of one's love, but the ring itself does not make you love the person more. Therefore, taking off the ring does not make you love any less. You are married only "until death do you part." So after one of you passes, your marriage obligations change. I finally realized I could love and be committed to her in a different way, like being there for her children and grandchildren.

Third, I had to at least be willing to entertain the idea that I could have a happy life again even though she was gone.

The fourth and final resolution, which was absolutely personal to me, was my uncertainty about whether the flowers on her grave would keep moving if I took off my ring. Well, that was a risk I was going to have to take because I was emotionally stuck in my grief. My ring had to come off, or I would be grieving for the rest of my life.

I decided that when I was finally able to remove my ring, I would wear it on a chain around my neck for a while as a transition phase. On January 1, 2011, I went to my wife's grave. This was the day I had picked to take off my wedding ring. The first day of the new year is the day a lot of us try to make a fresh start. We try to change our lives by overcoming vices or beginning a journey to achieve personal goals, many of which we have attempted and failed at so many times in the past. So that was the day I was going to once again attempt to do what so many people would see as something so easy, although I still found it to be an impossible task.

As I drove down the long lane leading off the country road to the cemetery where my wife was buried, I felt extremely nervous. At the entrance there was a stream with a narrow bridge wide enough for only one car to drive over. I drove over the bridge, just as I had many other times when I visited her grave site, but this time my stomach was in knots. The sun was out on that cold day, and the temperature was well below freezing. I parked the vehicle close to my wife's grave, got out, stepped onto the frozen ground, and shut the door. After the sound of the door closing, I heard total silence. I was all alone in that remote cemetery. The cold seemed to make the place even more isolated and quiet; not even a single bird was out to chirp.

I stood in front of her grave, told her I still loved her, and asked her to understand why I had to stop wearing my wedding ring. Then I took off my ring and put it on the chain around my neck. I continued to talk to her as I started to become emotional and tear up—but then I once again witnessed the wind blow and the flowers move. My wife had died on March 11, 2009. It had taken me one year and ten months to find the strength to remove my wedding ring.

As I drove back down the long lane leading to the country road, I wondered if those flowers would ever move for me again. I hoped my wife would not be mad at me. As I drove back across the one-lane bridge, I started to feel a warmth next to my skin underneath a locket that contained some of Elaine's ashes, which I also had on the chain around my neck. The closer I got to the road, the warmer the locket became. At first it felt like a heating pad on a low setting, but then it became very uncomfortable. I put my hand under my shirt, trying to feel what was wrong. I gripped the locket with one hand. The burning heat on my chest stopped, but the locket was cold. I let go of the locket, putting my hand back on the steering wheel. As the locket rested back on the center of my chest, again the heat started up. I felt the warmth penetrating my chest. There was no logical, scientific reason for this. I know that

Grief

this was Elaine telling me that she was not angry with me, and that the love we had for each other was in our hearts, not our rings. As I turned off the cemetery lane and drove down the main road, the heat stopped. I felt as if a huge weight had been lifted off of me. Finally, I no longer felt as if I were living a lie by continuing to wear my ring.

The next time I went to her grave, I looked at the flowers, and as usual, they moved! They still do each and every time I go there, even to this very day.

Surviving the Holidays

WHEN WE ARE STILL GRIEVING the loss of a loved one, we can start thinking about and dreading an upcoming holiday well before it actually arrives. Sometimes we do not have any expectations of joy; we want only to survive the day and get back to normal routines. Holidays can intensify our feelings of grief, putting us into deep sorrow to a point that we start to feel life has no value for us. In order to survive the holidays, we must understand what our heart needs. We need to be kind to ourselves; there is no reason to push ourselves into something we are not ready for. But we must also try to at least acknowledge the holidays, even though we are going to feel the pain of our loss. Going through the grieving process is hard enough on a normal day and extremely hurtful during holidays, but it is necessary if we want to eventually heal.

There are many holidays and we celebrate them for various reasons. Some holidays honor past presidents or people who have made significant contributions. Others are for remembrance of those who served in the military or who have lost their lives in battle. Then we have holidays that were created for social and economic reasons. Many countries have holidays that are specific to their heritage. There are also religious holidays with specific beliefs and celebrations that go along with them.

All relationships are different, and our grief is personal and unique to our relationship with the person we lost. Most people will celebrate holidays in traditional ways, but as our grief is personal, our holidays are also personal and unique to each of us and our families.

My oldest stepson was a big fan of the Ohio State football team, so naturally it became a tradition in our family to make sure he had a Christmas gift tagged to him from either the coach or a star player of the rival team of The Ohio State Buckeyes. Every year when he opened that gift, there would be either a hat or shirt with the logo of his team's mortal enemy, the Michigan Wolverines. Sometimes there would even be a rubber snake in the box. Then there was always a joke gift for his sister: a box inside many more boxes. These are just a couple of ways we made our Christmas unique and special for our family.

We all know Christmas and Easter are two major religious holidays in the Christian tradition, which millions of people celebrate every year. Of course, these two holidays have become so commercialized that even though many people celebrate the true religious meanings, the birth of Jesus as well as the resurrection of Jesus, a lot of us, especially those with young children, will indulge in the notion that there is a Santa Claus and an Easter Bunny. However, it does not matter if you have emphasized the true religious meaning or the commercialized aspect of a particular holiday, or even if you have done a combination of both. What matters is that someone you love is not going to be there this year because that person has died. That hurts, and it would put a damper on anyone's holiday. After all, seeing and being with the people we love is almost as important as the holiday itself.

My family always made big plans for Thanksgiving, Christmas, and Easter, so those three holidays were particularly hard for me to get through. My mother died in 2004, and I lost my wife in 2009. In both instances of loss, my grief increased during the holidays. However, when I lost my mother, I still had my father, my wife, my adult stepchildren, and my step-grandchildren. Even though I was very close to my mother and profoundly grieving her death, many other components of my life were still intact. This helped me get through my mother's death, because I did not feel like every facet of my life had been taken away.

A few days before my first Christmas without Mom, I felt so empty inside that I told a friend I did not care about the upcoming

GRIEF

Christmas. My wife's feelings were hurt when I said this! She had been so busy preparing for Christmas that she had not really noticed how bad I was feeling. But my wife told me that I still had her, as well as other family members who loved me. Still, I was grieving and did not want to celebrate, as I felt I could never be happy again.

During our Christmas celebration that year, the grandkids would approach me to show off one of their new toys. My wife was right—I had people around me who cared for me! Even though Christmas was emotionally painful, I got through the day with the support and love of my wife and others. And this was without having to make any changes in the way we celebrated the holiday.

However, my experience was not the same when my wife died. I had lost not just another part of my life, but the main component of my life. I also had many significant memories of not just the holidays, but also the time I had spent with her in preparation for the holidays. Christmas was absolutely the toughest holiday for me to deal with after my wife died because it was so important to her, and I had so many memories associated with our many Christmases.

Elaine did a Christmas like nothing I had ever seen. I believe anyone who saw it would have been impressed. I know there were many times I saw grandchildren walk into the living room and their little eyeballs almost popped out of their heads. Elaine probably had around two hundred gifts each year—one year she had three hundred gifts. We had them stacked under the tree and around the tree as high as three and a half feet. Plus, more gifts were stacked to the side and all the way down one of the walls in our living room. These gifts were divided among sixteen people in our large blended family. I was on board with this at first. I even bought a Santa Claus suit and pretended to be Santa. Elaine and I decided to let everyone have a chance to play Santa, so we started asking for volunteers. After the first four years of our family's Christmas holiday, everyone who wanted to be Santa had a chance. So we decided to give Santa a break until some of the very young grandchildren got a little older.

There was a lot of work and time involved in preparing for our big Christmas celebration, so eventually I asked Elaine to try to downsize some. I wanted her to give each of her three adult children $300 in cash. My thought was that if we spent $900 less on gifts, there would be much less shopping and wrapping, and this would surely make the work of preparing much easier. However, Elaine wanted a lot of presents under the tree, so she refused!

Elaine's Christmas Tree

Elaine was not a greedy or materialistic woman, so I did not understand why she was so determined to make our Christmas tree look like a Hallmark Christmas card. I just wanted the butler and maid to shop for the gifts and perform the hours upon hours of wrapping. But we did not have a butler or a maid. We had full-time jobs and a lot of other things that needed to be done. The only way we could afford to buy all those gifts was because Elaine would buy not only brand-new things, but also things that were in like-new condition from secondhand stores. My wife was a very wise shopper; we had an account set aside just for Christmas, which we added money to all year.

We did finally start doing some things to make the preparation a little easier. We began using a smaller tree that was not quite as difficult to put up. Elaine started to buy some of the pies and desserts pre-made. That did seem to make things a little easier, but not too much easier. There was still a lot of shopping and wrapping that needed to be done. Elaine would always tell me that she was going to downsize Christmas the next year. She never did! There were always just as many gifts to shop for and wrap as in past years. Elaine would use a week of her vacation time just to wrap gifts and do the baking and cooking. I would help her, but I had little patience for wrapping gifts; to me it was a boring job. One year I wrapped approximately seventy gifts. Each one was a mess, but I did not care because I had no desire to become a proficient gift wrapper. Elaine would tell me I was wasting paper, and then I would get even more aggravated. She did do most of the wrapping, but I helped her a lot with everything, even the shopping. We tried to get everything done a week before the celebration so we could have some time to relax.

I gave up on wanting her to downsize our Christmas. I had come to realize two things: One, Elaine was never going to downsize her Christmas, no matter what! Two, it made her happy, and I wanted her to be happy. Elaine told me it made her happy when her family opened gifts. She said seeing them surprised and happy when they opened their gifts was the greatest gift she could receive on Christmas Day.

Elaine gave hundreds of Christmas gifts over the years, including one that I did not know she had given until a year after she had died. I was talking with Elaine's daughter's ex-husband about Elaine. One of the grandsons was there, sitting on the floor, and I did not think he was paying much attention to our conversation. However, when he heard me say, "Elaine always had nice Christmases with lots of gifts for everyone," he looked our way and his face just lit up with joy. At that moment I knew Elaine had given him and everyone else a gift that would last a lifetime: the memories of beautiful Christmases with lots of gifts, lots of good food, and—what was most important to Elaine—lots of love and togetherness. Elaine's Christmas get-togethers were an expression of her love and kindness. They will never be forgotten!

After Elaine died, I knew I was never going to be able to mentally sustain my composure to prepare and sponsor the same kind of Christmas that she had always created. I could not even bear the thought of one of those elaborate Christmases without her, everyone opening gifts while I looked around our living room and saw no Elaine because she was dead! There was absolutely no way I was going to be able to handle that.

However, Elaine was very smart, and she knew me way too well. She knew I had a very high moral standard of following through with what I told people I would do. So she asked me to promise several things to her. One of them was that if anything ever happened to her, I would continue on with at least some kind of Christmas with her children and grandchildren. I also wanted to do this because even though my late wife's children and grandchildren were only my step children, I still cared for them and treated them like they were my biological children.

So I talked to my late wife's adult children about their mother's wish that we would continue to be a family and spend time together, especially during Christmas. They were very emotional; they told me they wanted me to remain in their lives. I let them know I would still buy Christmas gifts for them and the grandchildren, but unfortunately, with less income, I would not be able to buy as many. I explained how bad I felt, as just thinking about doing a Christmas in my house without their mother was very painful to me. I asked them if we could hold the gathering at one of their homes. Elaine's daughter also felt that she could not handle having the celebration in my house without her mother, so Elaine's oldest son volunteered to hold the gathering at his home.

    I did not really know it at the time, but the plan I had just set into motion was a key factor in helping me to survive my first Christmas without Elaine. A good way to help yourself get through a holiday is to think about what options you have and decide what you are going to do ahead of time. No general leads his army into a battle without some kind of a battle plan. Things might not go exactly as planned; he may have to deviate from and make adjustments to the original plan, but he knows his chances of winning the battle are far greater if he has a good strategy. By talking with my adult stepchildren about holding our Christmas celebration in a different place, I had taken the initial step in making a Christmas plan for myself. I then thought about and examined how other aspects of the holiday were going to affect me. I took some measures to deal with these issues to help me get through not only that day, but also the days leading up to the actual holiday. I incorporated into my plan not only what I was going to do, but also what I was not going to do! I knew it was best to avoid triggers for my grief.

    My plan for that first Christmas was simple: First, I would have the celebration in a place other than our house. Second, I would not put up a tree or any decorations in my house so I would not have to be reminded of Christmas on a daily basis. Third, I would try to avoid seeing any reminders of Christmas until it actually arrived. Fourth, I would go to my wife's grave and place some decorations there. I would tell her I loved her and let her know I would be spending time with her children and grandchildren, as I had promised.

Even though this plan helped, the first Christmas without my wife was so hard that I really cannot even find the words to describe how terrible I felt. I had to force myself every step of the way. I had bought about sixty gifts, far fewer than past years, but the wrapping was harder than it had ever been. This was not because I hated to wrap gifts, but because there was no Elaine. I was totally alone. I sat on the floor in my empty house, wrapping gifts and thinking about her. Eventually I broke down in tears.

The day of the Christmas get-together, I had a mixture of feelings. Sometimes I was sad and felt disconnected from everything that was going on around me. At other times I would be living in the moment and not thinking about anything else. This may sound strange, but at times I would feel like my late wife was there, even though she was dead. I had a feeling inside that was comforting to me. I did not know why I felt that way or where the feeling was coming from.

I believe that celebrating Christmas that first year with people who also loved Elaine was the best thing I could have done for myself. I was around others who were also grieving her death, which gave me a safe place where I could talk about her if I felt I needed to. And I did talk about her, and so did her children. We celebrated the holiday together, enjoying some happy moments but also sharing memories

Grief

of Elaine and consoling each other in our times of grief. After everything was over, on the drive back to my house, I thought about that feeling of comfort I had experienced. I realized my wife was there because each one of her children and grandchildren were a part of her; that was where those comforting feelings came from. Even though I had forced myself to take part in Christmas, the interaction with my blended family was exactly what I needed, and when I was around them, I felt a little better, like things were somewhat normal.

I never asked any of them, but my late wife's daughter told me on several occasions that she felt connected to her mother when she was around me. I was very fortunate to still be able to get along well with Elaine's adult children. So many times in a blended family, things go the opposite way. Don't think we haven't had our disagreements over the years, because we have. Yet we truly had become one family. Actually, my late wife's oldest son, daughter, and I became even closer after their mother passed away.

When the time came to celebrate the second Christmas after her death, I had made immense progress in my recovery; however, the grief still hit me hard that year. Even if you have arrived at a point of feeling a lot better and you seem to be functioning fine, a holiday can almost put your feelings in a time machine. That is exactly what happened to me—I went into a deep depression and became very angry. I felt the way I did when I first lost her. My feelings had regressed to where they had been a few months after her death, even though it had been almost two years. I did not feel that I could handle a long Christmas celebration, so I modified my previous year's Christmas plan to give myself a break.

My plan for the second Christmas without her would be as follows: First, I would not attend the family celebration. Instead, I would take the Christmas gifts to my late wife's adult children and grandchildren a few days before Christmas, visit with them for a while, and watch them open their gifts. Second, on Christmas Day I would stay home by myself. Then later that evening I would go to the movies with my stepson and his family. (Yes, most movie theaters are open on Christmas Day.) Third, I would continue to not put up any tree or decorations in my house so I would not constantly be reminded of Christmas.

That second year, my wife's daughter also could not make it to her brother's home because she had no transportation. She asked her brother to come get her, but he felt she lived too far away. In addition, the youngest son had not been attending any family functions after his mother's death, and he was also not living in the area, so it was impossible for him to attend. Since no one was able to come, my oldest stepson and his family did not host Christmas but instead went to his mother-in-law's house.

On Christmas Day I stayed home as I had planned. My thought was to have a quiet day to myself. I watched a Christmas sermon delivered by a TV preacher, took a nap, and then watched some other TV programs. Even though I was trying to keep my mind occupied, I was nervous all day. I had woken up that Christmas morning with my stomach in knots, and I felt extremely anxious the entire day. Even though I had previously felt like I should stay home, I was having second thoughts about my decision. Fortunately, I had made the plans to go to the movies that night, which helped. I was very happy to see my stepson and his family. They picked me up, we talked on the drive to the movie theater, and the nervous feeling I'd had all day went away. I realized it was a mistake for me to spend the day home alone that year. Sometimes we have to try what we think is best, and if we find out we made a bad choice, we simply make the necessary changes for the next year.

Unfortunately, by the time the third Christmas rolled around, my oldest stepson and his family had decided to celebrate Christmas with his wife's family. My daughter-in-law's mother did not want my daughter-in-law and stepson to sponsor the Christmas celebration. Because there were so many people in the family, the home would be crowded, and my daughter-in-law's mother thought one of the kids might get hurt during their wrestling and horseplay. My daughter-in-law's mother also wanted my daughter-in-law to uninvite certain family members. I think this put my daughter-in-law and oldest stepson in an awkward position. They did not want to hurt anyone's feelings, but they still wanted to maintain a favorable relationship with my daughter-in-law's mother. So for them, the easiest solution to dealing with this difficult situation without offending anyone was to no longer sponsor a large family gathering in their home. My daughter-in-law asked me if I wanted to come with them to her sister's house for Christmas. She said that her mother would probably not object. It was nice of my daughter-in-law to invite me to her family's celebration. I knew her parents and siblings and got along well with all of them. Yet based on some things that were said, I got the impression that the mother-in-law really wanted only her children and grandchildren there. So I thanked my daughter-in-law but declined the invitation.

I still did not feel like I could hold a Christmas celebration in my house; there were just way too many memories. And a part of me wanted those magnificent Christmases in our home to be associated only with Elaine. Because the situation had changed and my wife's adult children were no longer going to sponsor a large family get-together, there was no way we could continue to do a Christmas with the entire family like Elaine had hoped we could do. In order to keep my promise to my late wife, I would do the same thing I had done that second Christmas. I would go to the homes of each of her children a few days before Christmas and take their gifts to them and the grandchildren. Even though that was not quite what my wife had had in mind, at least I was letting my blended family know I cared about them.

The grandchildren were always happy to see me. They would run up to me and give me a hug. My adult stepchildren would greet me courteously. Although this was a perfectly acceptable interaction for a blended family, I was able to spend only about fifteen minutes with them, which did not feel like much of a Christmas to me. I felt more like a delivery man dropping off some gifts rather than part of the family. Something was missing.

We must remember that one of the things that matters the most to each of us, especially on a holiday, is spending time with people we love, feeling like we are loved, and being part of something.

I had become accustomed to spending several hours with a large group of people on Christmas. Even though I still had my elderly father, we were really not much comfort to each other. We usually ended up sitting in my living room on Christmas Day, looking at each other with nothing new to talk about. Although we tried to make the most of the day, we both would become bored. I would start thinking about my wife and mother both being deceased, and that made me feel miserable.

Nevertheless, I kept trying to make my Christmas a little better. One year I mailed out fifty-two real Christmas cards to family, friends, and acquaintances. You may wonder how that could have helped me in any way with my grief. Well, it gave me a task, something I needed to concentrate on, and it also helped me feel like I had some connections.

Grief

Whether the card was being sent to a friend or someone who was more of an acquaintance, what was important to me was that the people who received the cards knew I had thought enough of them to take time to send a card. I even got some cards back, which can really help you feel better. I also passed out Christmas cards to some people who worked in the local Walmart, because I liked them and they were always nice to me. I also started giving out small, inexpensive gifts to people I interacted with on a professional level, because I valued them and considered them to be my friends. Doing small things like these did help me to acknowledge the holiday. Even so, it was still always a challenge for me to find ways to be happy during Christmas.

Thanksgiving was not much better. In most of the grief groups I attended, there always seemed to be someone who would advise those people with no place to go to volunteer at community-sponsored dinners. I fully understand the philosophy behind that recommendation, and I have helped others, especially when I was dealing with a lot of my own problems. However, I just did not feel that standing in a serving line, dishing out food, was going to help me feel any better. I already felt like I was being punished—my wife had been taken away from me.

We are all different, so if serving others in that way gives you some relief, by all means, volunteer. My dad had talked me into going to some community-sponsored Thanksgiving dinners, dinners for people who had no place to go on Thanksgiving. The majority of people there were either homeless or were having some financial problems. Please understand that I am a very down-to-earth person, and I in no way thought anything bad about the people who were attending those dinners. But I was angry that I had no other place to go.

One year, Dad and I were seated beside a man and his wife who were not homeless, but one of them had recently lost a job. They were complaining about paying taxes. I have a sense of humor and a bit of an ornery streak in me, so I told them I had not paid taxes in the last ten years. They asked me if I had been jobless for ten years. I said, "No, I have a job. I just do not pay any taxes!" I was just joking, but these people did not know me. The man asked me my name, and I told him I never gave out my name after I'd just told a stranger I did not pay taxes. They gave me a very apprehensive look. My dad told them I was just joking, and we all laughed. The man then said that if I had truly not paid taxes, he would not blame me. He went on to say that he had cheated on his taxes, and if he would ever be audited, he would probably owe the government thousands of dollars. I asked him his name, and he told me. Then I asked him how to spell his last name, and he told me how to spell it. I then asked him what his address was.

He gave me a strange look and said, "Why do you want my address?"

I replied, "Because I work for the IRS!"

Everyone at the table started laughing. The guy was speechless. My dad was laughing too, but immediately told everyone that I did not work for the IRS. Then the guy started laughing himself. We actually had a very good time that year. All four of us laughed and joked around the whole time we were there. The following year Dad and I went back, but our newfound tax-cheating friends were not in attendance.

Going to those sponsored Thanksgivings eventually started to feel degrading to me, not because there were homeless people there, but because the people volunteering would always run up to my dad and more or less ask who we were and why we were there. And he would tell them! There was nothing wrong with that—I just felt like it was a little humiliating to have to tell people that my mother and my wife had both died and we had no place to go for Thanksgiving. Finally, I decided I did not want to go anymore, and we stopped going.

Although the holidays are hard for anyone who has lost a loved one, those who have caring, supportive families usually have some place to go. Those who do not, can find themselves feeling lonely and abandoned as if no one cares. Hearing friends, coworkers, and acquaintances talk about their holiday plans does not help and can make you start to feel like an outcast from society. A person can even start to re-evaluate life and think that life cannot really be all that meaningful without even one friend or family member to gather with. Even if a person wants to stay home and ignore the holiday, it still feels better to be invited to a holiday celebration. At least it gives the feeling of having some options. Over the years, sometimes I was invited to a holiday celebration but turned down the invitation, only to change my mind several times before I finally decided to go. So if someone does invite you, and you are 100 percent sure you want to stay home, politely decline by saying that you do not feel like celebrating—but also ask if you could still come if you change your mind. Doing this leaves the door open just in case you do change your mind. As for myself, even though I was set on doing nothing on some holidays, just knowing I had someplace to go if I wanted to helped me feel better. Often, by the time the holiday arrived, my mood had improved enough that I was able to go.

Families in America are not normally as close as some other cultures. The family unit is more or less the parents, children, and grandparents. I had no siblings, but one of my cousins knew how badly the holidays affected me, so he invited Dad and me to his home for a few Thanksgivings and even a Christmas. Being around some biological family, whom I had known my whole life, gave me a sense of belonging. There were also children there, opening gifts and playing with their Christmas toys, which always creates fun. That was a Christmas very much like what I was used to having when my wife was alive. It was very kind of my cousin to invite us.

I have found that family and friends are likely to think of someone who is grieving on Christmas and Thanksgiving, but totally forget about the person on other holidays. For me, the Fourth of July was also a very hard holiday. Over the years there were ups and downs with all of my holidays, but Independence Day was tremendously gloomy for me. That was completely my fault for intentionally planning on doing nothing on the Fourth. I just gave up on that day.

I did this for two reasons. The first reason was that I was angry that my wife was not there with me for the Fourth of July. This anger was a little more complicated than one might see on the surface. After my mother passed away in 2004, I did not want to see fireworks. My mom loved fireworks, so for me, seeing fireworks stirred up emotions I was not ready to deal with. My wife was fine with us not doing anything special on the Fourth of July. Her adult children and grandchildren normally spent that holiday with her ex-husband. My wife preferred we work on this day anyway and save the holiday double-time pay for Christmas. However, in January 2009, I talked to my wife and made plans to attend a large fireworks display in our state's capital for the upcoming Independence Day that year.

My wife died in March of 2009. Needless to say, I did not attend that fireworks display in July or any other fireworks display for many years. The second reason I refused to make any effort on the Fourth of July was because I knew my family and friends were having cookouts and going to see fireworks, but no one ever invited me. I felt that if no one cared about me enough to ask me to join them, I was not going to beg them to let me tag along. This was not completely rational thinking. The truth is, a lot of people get so wrapped up in their own lives that they seldom think about anything other than what pertains to them. Even if some of them truly did not care about me, so what?! I should not have let this affect me so badly. I was making things way worse than they had to be.

The second Fourth of July after my wife's death was so bad that I truly wanted to just die myself. I felt my life was completely hopeless. I just lay in bed with the curtains pulled. The next-door neighbor was having a cookout, and after sunset I could hear firecrackers and bottle rockets. Every time I heard one explode, I felt as though my stomach was in knots. I was so despondent that I went to sleep that night and prayed to God, asking him to just let me die in my sleep. Some people can view a statement like this with a condescending attitude. But the reality is that when people feel their lives are completely hopeless, they can feel like giving up, and thoughts of suicide might even enter into some people's minds. Thoughts like these are one thing, but acting on those thoughts is another. You do not want to let the holidays get you so down that you get into this frame of mind.

Remember to consider that there are three-hundred and sixty-five days in a year. You have made it to this holiday, and tomorrow will be just another normal day. So, no matter how bad you may feel, you can get through the day. You are not the only person in the world who is feeling sad. Even people who have not experienced a recent loss can become extremely depressed on a holiday. We have to try to be content and make the most out of our day. Making some kind of plan is an extremely important part of giving ourselves a chance to have a happier day. When I developed the mindset of refusing to do anything on the Fourth of July, this was the absolute worst possible thing I could have ever done.

I finally realized my mistake, and after many years of doing nothing, I began making some plans for an upcoming Fourth of July holiday. I had lunch with a good friend, I bought myself a pair of sandals, I swam in the afternoon, and for the first time in many years, I went to a fireworks display with some family members. The next day my father and I went to see a movie, and I swam some more. Knowing what I was going to do was certainly a lot better than walking around feeling like I had no connections and nothing to do.

In my journey through my grief, I have handled my holidays in different ways. I have made plans for some holidays, and I have stayed home with no plans for other holidays, totally disregarding them. Yet no matter how bad I was feeling, I would always be in a better frame of mind when I had something to do or spent some time with people I felt comfortable with.

I know this is not always possible, and if it is not, we just have to experiment and keep trying things out until we find what works for us. If you have recovered from your grief enough that you feel like you could enjoy a vacation, don't rule that out. In December 2016, seven years after my wife's death, I traveled to Macau, China. It was the first time in my life that I had been out of the United States. I even had to overcome my fear of flying to make the twenty-one-hour flight. But I did it! I landed in Hong Kong and took the ferry to Macau. While I was there, I stood on a beach halfway around the world, put my bare feet in the ocean, placed my hand on the ruins of Saint Paul's, walked through a historical military fort, ate traditional Chinese foods, watched parades, and saw many interesting things. The many Christmas lights and decorations in China did not bother me. Seven years had passed since my wife's death, and I had overcome my grief.

One evening I was watching an amazing water show—the water would spout several stories into the air, and lights illuminated the spray. As the height of the water changed, the colors of the lights also changed and music played. Suddenly the song "My Heart Will Go On" by Celine Dion started to play. You know what? I thought about my late wife and I started to tear up, but I closed my eyes for a few seconds so no one would know.

Then, as if I were saying a prayer, I silently spoke to Elaine. I wished her a Merry Christmas and told her I loved her. I let her know I was doing everything she asked me to do. I opened my eyes, wiped away a tear, and went with some friends to ride the cable cars.

We need to try to think positively about our holidays and live our lives the best we can, whether the plan is to travel to China or just go to Walmart and buy a new pair of sandals. The bottom line is that surviving the holidays is hard, but we must have hope that things will get better.

I am sorry for your loss, and I hope you not only survive your holidays but find joy in them once again. I hope this chapter has encouraged you to look for ways to feel happy on your holidays.

Building a New Life

WHEN SOMEONE WE LOVE DIES, we must start to build a new life—one that does not include that person. This is by no means an easy task. Although much will change due to circumstances beyond our control that will take us in new directions that we might never have gone on our own, we have to knowingly put some effort into constructing a new life for ourselves. There were many times I felt like giving up; I was in an extremely low place emotionally.

Grief

One could say I was not even on level ground but in a deep pit of sorrow and depression. When I was finally able to pull myself out of my depression enough to attempt putting my life back together, I would often again fall into a hopeless mindset and become severely depressed. You have to keep in mind that you will never totally recover from your loss, but eventually you will feel normal again. You will experience many highs and lows before you feel like you have a meaningful life once more. But at some point in your life, you can be happy even though the person you loved is no longer there. So no matter how awful things may seem to be, do not give up!

Recovering from grief is like a roller-coaster ride. Our emotions will be up and down the same way a roll coaster goes up and down. If you have ever ridden on a roller coaster, I am sure the slow trek up the first hill, along with the clicking noise from the chains pulling you to the top, made you feel a little nervous. If you have a fear of heights, you might have even become terrified. After you reach the top of the first hill, by no means is the journey completed. Next, you will drop very fast, racing to the bottom only to face more intense hurdles with many ups and downs, twists and turns, and possibly loops or tunnels waiting for you. At times you might think the car you are riding in will fly off the track and you will not survive. Nevertheless, there can be some moments when you feel everything is okay and you are excited about what will come next.

When we are grieving, we are riding an emotional roller coaster. There will be times when we feel like we are not going to survive. Then we will start to have hope and feel like everything is going to be okay, only to be thrust back into a state of despair. Something that was very helpful to me was looking into new activities that I thought I might like—for example, scuba diving or playing a musical instrument. Most of the things I checked on I could not do because of my own health issues, time constraints, or finances. At first, everything I could think of was not suitable for me due to various reasons. Actually, that was okay! What mattered was that I was giving myself a break from thinking about my loss. During these short intervals of time, not only was my mind off of my situation, but subconsciously I was engaged in the notion that I could have a life without my wife. If you are like me, you may feel that you are not able to enjoy a new hobby, especially if your loss is recent. However, there is no harm in just looking into activities that you think you might want to try in your future. Finding a new hobby can be a challenge, and it might take you a while to find something you are truly interested in.

If you are still working a full-time job, or have some other obligations, a large portion of your day may already be accounted for. I am not saying you have to dedicate a lot of your free time to something new just to distract yourself from your loss. But if you can merely find one new thing that you are truly interested in, you will have taken a significant step in building a new life for yourself.

I checked on many different options before I committed to doing something new on a regular basis. I simply began to rebuild my life by forcing myself to do small things that did not require any future commitments, like going to a sporting event or car show. Although I was familiar with these kinds of activities, I did not necessarily do them with my late wife. When possible, I would engage in a conversation with a stranger about current events, or anything I could think of, just so I would not feel so disconnected and alone. Occasionally I would also take the grandchildren to a movie, as this gave me a chance to spend time with them and kept me from sitting at home all by myself.

GRIEF

Eventually I did start moving out of my comfort zone by engaging in some new activities that were completely different from anything I had ever done in my life. This helped me to focus on the present, not my past and my loss. Adding new endeavors to your life is a key factor in building a new life. When I talk about building a new life, I do not mean changing every facet of your life, only making some new and positive changes.

When we lose a loved one, we automatically have a new life, but not a life we ever wanted. Even if we have worked through a lot of our grief and have started to accept what has happened, our life is still not going to feel normal because the person we loved is no longer around. If that person was directly or indirectly involved in many of our activities and routines, those things are just not going to feel the same anymore. When we are doing something completely different from anything we had previously done with our lost loved one, we will not have memories associated with that person and the new activity.

We may still feel a little strange to be doing something without our loved one, but eventually this will pass. As we continue to engage in our new hobby or activity on a regular basis, we create a "new normal" in our life. If we are passionate about what we are doing, we may tend to think about how we can improve or reach our personal goals concerning these new interests. This will definitely help us feel like we have a normal life once again, as we will be giving not only our time but also our thoughts to something we enjoy.

With the passing of time, I worked through a lot of my grief, but my life still did not feel completely normal until I started working consistently on taking care of myself. I had to learn how to do this because I am a person who tends to look out for others more than I do myself. However, my wife, who had been a huge part of my life, was gone, and without her there was no way my life could feel normal. I had to make myself the key component of my life. Now, I am not saying I stopped looking out for other family members or that I had to become a selfish person. What I did have to do was begin to take steps to improve my life and start doing things I enjoyed.

Pursuing enjoyment will make life better for anyone, but especially for someone who has suffered a loss. Ask yourself these questions: What do I enjoy doing? What makes me happy? What have I always wanted to try but never attempted? Is there a personal goal I have always wanted to achieve? Is there anything I want to change about myself, such as overcoming a fear or phobia, or dropping a bad habit? Focusing your attention on improving yourself, and on what makes you happy, will definitely take your life in many new directions.

Before your loved one passed away, you may have been perfectly satisfied with your life just the way it was. But there is always room to grow and add something new. Alternatively, if you used to really enjoy something that now triggers your grief, you may want to try to change something about that activity. For example, I loved to swim, but unfortunately swimming at home in the same pool I used to swim in with my wife would trigger my grief. So I began a regimen of swimming in a completely different environment by going to a large indoor pool. This made it possible for me to enjoy swimming without triggering my grief, and I even made some new friends.

My entire life I have had a phobia of high places, which always left me standing around at amusement parks while others enjoyed going on the rides—not to mention the fact that there were many places I could never go on vacation because the thought of getting on an airplane horrified me. I wanted to overcome this fear, so I began watching fear-of-flying videos and took some classes on relieving anxiety through pressure points. Next, I bought a season pass to a nearby theme park purely for enjoyment. With the help of some family members, I was able to work my way up to riding some of the taller roller coasters. This allowed me to overcome my fear of heights enough to take the trip to China that I previously mentioned. I never dreamed I would be able to travel that far, going halfway around the world by flying on three airplanes. For someone who was terrified of heights, this was a huge accomplishment. I still have a fear of high places, but I keep working on it and no longer let my phobia stop me from doing what I truly want to do. I have no desire to skydive, as I am sure I would suffer a heart attack before I made it to the ground, but I am proud of myself for what I have been able to achieve.

I also started taking some classes once a week at a learning center that helps people learn a wide range of skills. I wanted to improve my spelling and writing. I made the decision that, in spite of my dyslexia, I would write this book in the hope that it would help others who are grieving.

Although I set some really big goals, which required a lot of dedication and hard work, I was also kind to myself by adding things to my life that took little or no effort. This is very important—we need to just have fun and relax sometimes. I felt relieved to once again be able to sit in my living room and watch TV without being overwhelmed by grief. I would sit by an open window, enjoying the cool breeze, as I watched a new television series about a criminal who had become an informant for the FBI. If you can find new shows that keep you on the edge of your seat to replace the shows you used to watch with your loved one, this will be a huge help.

People may suggest that you do some kind of volunteer work. I think this is fine, but I would recommend finding something that not only is helpful to others but also incorporates something that you are interested in. Remember that you are the one who needs the extra kindness. If you like animals, you might consider volunteering at an animal shelter or some kind of rescue operation. If you love sports and are like me, too old and beat up to participate, you may look into coaching a kids' team. Speaking of kids, I used to make my grandchildren laugh by talking to them with a puppet, which I named Alvin Alligator. As I am young at heart, I had fun doing this, so I also considered learning ventriloquism and possibly visiting hospitals to cheer up sick children. I never followed through with this, but at some point in my future when the time is right, I will.

You don't have to have huge accomplishments or do over-the-top, elaborate activities to feel happy. You may never climb Mount Everest, but that does not mean you cannot become an avid hiker who enjoys nature and looks forward to the next trail. But do not limit yourself in what you want to do with your life. In spite of your loss, try to look forward to your future and have the courage to follow your dreams. Try to think positively, keep hope in your heart, and believe that life has good things waiting for you. Be kind to yourself and be patient! Believe you will have happiness in your future.

Dating Again

THIS CHAPTER IS ABOUT some concerns I had before I started dating again and how I worked through these issues. I believe you must be positive and open-minded before beginning to date. If you have not worked through at least some of your grief, the chances of finding someone and being able to make that relationship work will be very slim. Any relationship is hard enough without including your unresolved issues. This does not mean you need to be completely over a loss; we are never 100 percent over something so tragic as the death of our spouse. Before you start dating, you should give some serious thought to how it could affect you in not only favorable but also unfavorable ways.

Love is a very powerful emotion, and there are different kinds of love. We love our parents, children, and spouses, but in different ways and for different reasons. What makes each of us fall in love with our spouse? Why did we fall in love with that certain person? To answer these questions, we must be able to answer the basic question, *What is love?* Maybe love is really beyond human understanding. The phrase "true love" can mean something different for everyone. True love to me is when a man is thinking about a woman and missing her. I believe that a man who truly loves a woman always wants to spend time with her, for no other reason than wanting to see her smile, look into her eyes, and hear her voice. He worries about her when she is sick. He does things to surprise her because he wants to make her happy. Just before he falls asleep at night, barely still awake, he reaches over and pats her to make sure she is still there. He looks at her from a distance and he is not able to take his eyes off her. When they visit family or friends and it is time to go, he feels fortunate that she is leaving with him. He puts her first before anything or anybody else. He finds himself doing things he does not want to do just because he wants to make her happy. He tells her he is sorry when he is wrong, and now and then he apologizes even when she is wrong. Even if he is angry at her, he knows he never truly wants to be without her. He works to learn and understand her mind and heart. When a man does all of these things for a woman, and she in turn does the same for him, and they both appreciate each other's gestures, this is true love.

Most grief groups that I have attended discuss dating. Some show videos, which usually say very little. Often someone who has lost his or her spouse will speak up, asking how and where to meet someone. A lot of times, people are still grieving but are lonely and start thinking maybe they can possibly find true love again. Many are not really ready to date, or thinking clearly, and they may even feel guilty about having such thoughts. Loneliness is not a reason to jump into a relationship. Your life was torn apart by the death of someone you deeply loved. A bad dating experience or relationship will compound the grief of your loss. There is no set amount of time that needs to pass before you start dating. From what I have seen, a lot of people will start dating between one and two years after the loss, but I have seen some date as soon as six months after. I personally did not go on a date until three and a half years after my wife passed. That was how much time I needed to deal with my grief. I am glad I waited that long, because when I went on that first date, I did not have any unresolved grief issues. However, I did make the mistake of letting my expectations become way too high, which in turn caused me a lot of heartache. Just make sure that when you do start to date, you are able to do so without guilt or high expectations. Every grief group facilitator will tell you to be careful about dating.

I am going to be very blunt about my experiences with dating. To be straightforward, I found it difficult to find dating partners who didn't lie! This can be shocking and hurtful, as some people are very deceitful and they lie convincingly. They are malicious and will try to use you. They will seem to be genuinely interested and caring; however, they may be interested only in sex or in scamming you out of your money. A person's true intentions will be revealed only with time.

GRIEF

There are also many people who only want to casually date. If they are honest about their objective, we should respect them for being truthful. Then we can determine whether or not to continue seeing them based on the facts. On the other hand, when people enter into a relationship with miscommunication, it is very likely someone will have hard feelings or be brokenhearted. So be thankful if your date is honest enough to tell you what he or she is truly looking for; this may save both of you some time and pain.

You may also encounter people who are searching for love but do not know what true love is. They may be unable to recognize or appreciate truly good qualities in another person, and they may have undesirable character traits, like being selfish, critical, controlling, arrogant, unfaithful, exceedingly materialistic, or being unable to stay committed. If you become involved with someone who has one or more of these negative attributes, the relationship may be unhealthy for you and doomed to fail.

Even if you have entered into a relationship with a caring person who has good morals, that person's life may just be going in a different direction from yours. Or you might find that the person you have started to date is just not a good match for you. For those of us who have lost our spouses, it is vital not to let our expectations get too high in a new relationship. Most of the time, relationships do not work out even if they have started on a positive note. Try to keep your emotions in check and take things slowly—although that can be easier said than done, especially if you are lonely.

I am absolutely not an expert on dating. But I have unjustly had my heart broken by fake people on more than one occasion. So I would suggest that you try to date someone you have personally known for a while. However, if that is not possible, try to find someone who has had some of the same life experiences as you, or someone who has some of the same hobbies and interests. If both of you are into something that happens to be a key component of your life, then you may have a good foundation to begin building a sound relationship. However, it can be hard to find that special person you can have a meaningful and lasting relationship with. So do not make things more difficult by letting preconceived notions, or unresolved grief, be the reason you miss out on finding true love.

When you start dating, you need to have an open heart and mind. While I was attending grief groups, I heard some people talk about their late spouses as though they were perfect, putting them on such a high pedestal that no one could ever be as good as they were. They would even make bold statements like, "We never had so much as one argument in the whole twenty years." Even if that were true, anyone who is going to start dating needs to be honest and admit that no one is perfect. If in your mind your late spouse was flawless, then you are not being fair to the person you are presently dating, or to yourself. Realistically, ask yourself these questions: Was my marriage great because my late spouse was perfect, or was my marriage great because we both worked to make the marriage awesome? Or did my late spouse's imperfections just not matter to me?

When I started to think about dating, an acquaintance told me, "You will never find anyone who can replace Elaine, [and] if you looked the world over, never again will you have that kind of love." You may feel this way if you recently lost your spouse, and there is nothing wrong with this. However, if you begin dating in an attempt to find true love, this is an incorrect mindset. Personally, I never thought of dating as a search to replace what I had lost. Each one of us is unique and can never be replaced. Also, your love for your deceased spouse was very special and distinct. Elaine was an immensely kind woman; I think of her often and will love her forever. I never ever thought having a relationship with another woman would replace my late wife or diminish what I once had with her in any way. However, I knew that with the right woman I could have an even better relationship than the one I had with my late wife, because of what I had learned from my marriage to Elaine. I was able to communicate and understand things much better. So when I began dating, I did so with a willingness to build a new relationship that would be even better than the one I had with my late wife.

Over the years I have seen people who have lost a spouse go on countless dates only to immediately find something wrong and nitpick. If you do this, you will be sabotaging any chance you have of finding true love. If you have been dating someone for a while and decide to stop, make sure you have a legitimate reason, and if possible, respectfully share it with the person.

If you do find that special person and enter into a committed relationship, you may have to deal with some jealousy issues. I am not talking about your new love being jealous of one of your coworkers, or the salesperson at the mall who seemed to be extra friendly. You may be surprised to find that sometimes there can be jealousy toward your late spouse. This may sound peculiar, but I have experienced it and observed it in others. The person you are dating may occasionally wonder if you love him or her as much as you loved your late spouse. Also, in the beginning of your new relationship, your date may be curious and ask some questions about your late spouse, but I caution you to not bring up your late spouse in conversation too much. The new person in your life really does not want to hear about your late spouse any more than you would want to hear your date talking about his or her ex all the time. I am not saying you can never mention your late spouse's name, but just try to be mindful of your new love's feelings. I suggest that if the name of your late spouse happens to come up, you add something to the conversation about how important the new person in your life is to you. The bottom line is that if you are in a relationship with someone who is jealous of your late spouse, both of you will need to talk things over and come to some compromise. This issue does not have to become a huge problem.

On a lighter note, I have a funny story to share. A buddy of mine who had also lost his wife got remarried. The woman he married would ask him which person he loved more, his late wife or her. Even though he told her many times that he loved both of them the same, she was not willing to accept his answer. One day she said, "Well, let me ask you this: if your late wife and I both fell into a pit of lions and you could save only one of us, who would you save?"

My buddy, who was an all-around decent guy, and who also had a sense of humor, replied, "I have told you over and over again: I love both of you the same, so I would not be able to pick. I would let the lions eat both of you." To end her relentless interrogation, he continued, "But if you ask me one more time, I am going to save her and let the lions eat you." Both of them would start laughing, as obviously this issue was no longer a problem for them.

Ultimately, there are many challenges ahead of us when we begin dating or start a new relationship. Yet before we enter into the dating world, there are two important issues that must be examined: unfounded guilt and how dating will affect our relationship with our families.

A lot of people will feel guilty when they began dating, especially if they deeply loved their spouse. But our marriage vows

GRIEF

say we are married "until death do us part." Therefore, to start dating again is not cheating or being disrespectful. We need to give ourselves permission to look for love again. In our hearts we must truly feel that we are not doing anything wrong. In my case, I got a break because my late wife made me promise that I would get remarried if anything ever happened to her. This was an exceedingly kind and selfless act on her part. She loved me enough to allow me the opportunity to not be alone after she was gone. But even if she and I had not discussed this topic, I believe I knew her well enough to know that she would not have wanted me to grieve her death for the rest of my life.

Remember that if you love someone, it hurts you to see that person in pain. I do not believe your deceased spouse would want you to be lonely for the rest of your life. Wouldn't he or she want you to find someone who could make you smile again, someone who cherishes you, shares happy times with you, and stays by your side to comfort you if you were to be sad or get sick? If you know your spouse loved you, don't you think he or she would want you to search for love with his or her blessing and without guilt? If you answer yes to these questions, then you owe it to yourself and your late spouse to search for true love.

Another issue that needs to be considered is how dating might affect family members. What will their reactions be? Will it be one of approval or anger? Unfortunately, this can be a complicated situation that may not turn out as you had hoped. I feared that if I started dating, my adult stepchildren might think I did not love their mother. I had always had a very good relationship with my oldest stepson and his family. My wife's daughter and I, on the other hand, had some disputes in the beginning, but eventually we resolved our differences and became close. I was mindful not to destroy the relationships I had built with my late wife's children.

One thing I had learned from Elaine was that sometimes you need to put yourself in the other person's place before you say or do anything. I decided I was going to start dating, but I wanted to talk to my adult stepchildren about it. I wanted them to know I respected their feelings. I asked how they felt about my decision, and I observed their initial reaction. Sometimes the best approach to informing others about a major change is to give them a chance to get used to the idea. If I had gotten a negative reaction, I planned on just letting the subject drop and discussing it further at a later time. Luckily, I did not have to do this as they were very understanding and fully supportive of me. Because I was not their biological dad, they may have found it easier to accept my dating. Of course, they also could have gotten upset and cut all ties with me. I needed to be willing to accept whatever would happen, and you need to do the same.

If your children seem to be opposed to you having someone new in your life, hopefully when they see how happy you are they will reach a level of acceptance. I feel the only people we ever have any obligation to seek approval from are our children. However, ultimately, we must do what is best for ourselves. We love our children—they are a big part of our lives—but we also deserve to have a happy, fulfilling life ourselves.

No one has a right to say that you should not be dating or to pass judgment on you. I have heard nosy busybodies gossip and say some nasty things about someone who has started dating. No decent person should do this, but this kind of thing can make us fear what our own friends or even acquaintances may think about us. You will find that your true friends, and even some acquaintances, will be

GRIEF

happy to see you dating. They may have even been worried about you and are glad to see you trying to go on with your life.

Dating is not for everyone! I have seen people in grief groups who came right out and said that they had no desire to ever date. These people will merely choose to devote their remaining time with their existing family and friends, and that is fine.

If you do decide to search for true love, I wish you the best of luck! I hope that after reading this chapter, you will search with an open heart and mind, but also with a great deal of caution.

Who Is Elaine?

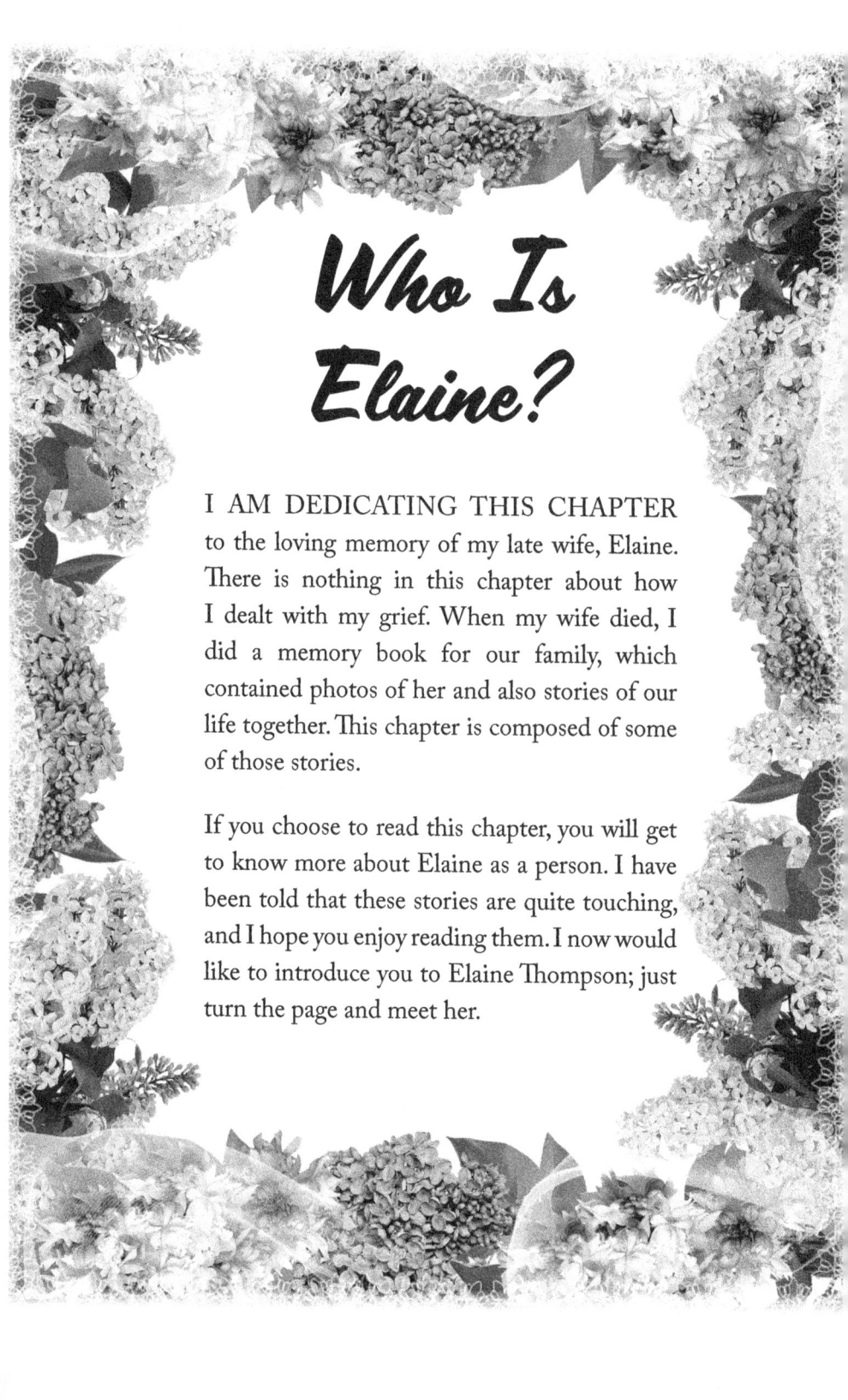

I AM DEDICATING THIS CHAPTER to the loving memory of my late wife, Elaine. There is nothing in this chapter about how I dealt with my grief. When my wife died, I did a memory book for our family, which contained photos of her and also stories of our life together. This chapter is composed of some of those stories.

If you choose to read this chapter, you will get to know more about Elaine as a person. I have been told that these stories are quite touching, and I hope you enjoy reading them. I now would like to introduce you to Elaine Thompson; just turn the page and meet her.

GRIEF

Elaine's Christmas Eagle

The bald eagle represents strength, courage, and freedom. If you have ever seen one up close, you know why the eagle was picked to be the national bird of the United States. On our way to work, Elaine and I would drive by a house where a man made and sold wood carvings. He had several of them on display in his front yard, and most of them were eagles. Every time Elaine and I went by that house, Elaine told me how much she liked those carvings. She would always say, "Those eagles are so neat."

One summer, in late June, Elaine's youngest son called me. He asked me if I thought his mother would like to have one of those eagles. I told him that Elaine absolutely loved those eagles. He asked me if I would buy one and let him make payments to me. He wanted to give the eagle to his mother for Christmas. I agreed to do this for him, so I bought an eagle. I put the heavy, three-foot carving in our garage and covered it with a blanket. Not only was I excited about the fact that Elaine was going to get one of those eagles, but I also knew that this Christmas gift, coming from her youngest son, would make Elaine very happy.

Elaine and I were sitting in the living room one evening watching TV. I just had to ask her, "If we ever did someday get one of those carved eagles, where would we put it?" Elaine was not too enthusiastic about even discussing the eagle, much less figuring out a spot in which to put the statue. I kept talking about the subject, and then Elaine blurted out, "I don't care. If you buy one, put the eagle wherever you want. I don't even like them!"

I was shocked. "What do you mean you don't like them?! For the last two years, we rode past that house where the guy sells them, and you have told me how nice they are and how much you liked them."

Elaine replied, "I do like them, but for you, not me. I like butterflies!"

I felt sick when she said this, and I did not know what to do. I finally told her that her son wanted to get her one for Christmas, and I had told him that she liked them. Elaine said, "Tell him not to get me one. I think they are ugly."

I told her I could not do that.

"Why not?" she said.

I replied, "Because we already got the eagle. It is in the garage, waiting for Christmas!" Elaine started to laugh, but I did not think this was funny.

I asked her what we were going to do. She replied, "You mean what *you* are going to do. You are the one who told him I like those ugly eagles." Elaine could see I did not think this was funny, so she finally said, "I'll act like I like eagles when I open it."

I wrapped the eagle the morning of our Christmas get-together. It ended up being a gift from both her youngest son and me, since we both had money in this ugly, well-carved eagle. Elaine and I looked at each other just before she opened this Christmas gift.

We did not say a word, but our eyes had a definite conversation. We were the only two people in the room who knew the whole story about this odd-looking, sloppily wrapped gift.

Elaine acted surprised and told her son she loved the eagle. I think that made him feel good, and he looked happy. After everyone went home, Elaine hugged and kissed me. Then she said, "Thank you for the eagle."

"I thought you said those eagles were ugly?"

"Not this one. My son, whom I love, thought of me and wanted to give me a Christmas gift. My husband, whom I love, helped my son do this. That eagle came from two people I love, so it is not ugly! It is the most beautiful eagle that will ever be carved."

Who is Boo?

Elaine and I were married in August, and in October of that year we went to a flea market where she saw a small ghost on an arts and crafts table. The ghost was made of cloth and straw and was approximately seven inches tall with the word *Boo* written across the front. Elaine could be tight with money and did not want to pay the amount the seller was asking, so even though she wanted this Halloween decoration, she refused to make the purchase. On our way back to the car, I told her I had to go to the restroom and would meet her at the car. Instead, I went to the crafts table and bought that ghost for her. I hid the ghost in the back seat of our car. Later that evening I surprised her with the gift.

We named the ghost Boo, after the word written across his chest. Boo was placed in our living room on the mantel over the fireplace. He seemed to like that spot—well, Elaine and I liked him there anyway. We joked around a lot with each other, pretending like Boo was real. Boo never did talk to us, but we talked to him! When we were ready to go to bed, we would turn off the TV and the lights, leave the living room, and tell Boo goodnight. Whenever one of us went someplace alone, we would leave a note and sign the bottom with the phrase "Boo, I love you." Then we started placing that seven-inch-tall ghost on top of our notes as a paperweight. Sometimes we would place him in other rooms in the house just to tease each other. Boo was passed around our home hundreds of times throughout our marriage, traveling from room to room. Sometimes he would get lost and we would ask each other, "Hey, do you know where Boo is?"

We even started to use the word *boo* as a secret way to say "I love you." No one else knew that "boo" meant "I love you." We both had to laugh when one of the grandkids would get ready to leave the house, give us a hug, and say, "I love you," and we would slip up and reply with just, "Boo." After Elaine died, I realized how much passing Boo back and forth meant to me. I still have Boo; he is stored in a box. When I stored him away, I thought I might give him to one of the grandchildren someday. But I have decided to keep Boo until the day I die.

Elaine's Elvis Bear

Elaine and I were just friends at work when Elaine had her heart attack. I went to visit her while she was in the hospital and brought her some paperback books and a little stuffed bear that had sunglasses on. Elaine liked that stuffed bear. She said the bear reminded her of Elvis Presley because it was wearing sunglasses like a rock star. Elaine even gave the stuffed bear the name Elvis. After Elaine got out of the hospital, we started to date and eventually got married. For our honeymoon, we planned on visiting several places in North Carolina and Tennessee. After seeing a program on the Travel Channel about Elvis Presley and

GRIEF

Graceland, even though Elaine was not really an Elvis fan, we decided to add Memphis, Tennessee, with a tour of Graceland, to our list of places to visit. That program taught us that Priscilla Presley never got remarried after she and Elvis divorced. Elaine liked that a lot—her face just lit up when she heard this. As we watched the Travel Channel showing home movies of the Presleys sledding in the snow, Elaine said, "Priscilla Presley loved Elvis; that's why she never got remarried!" Then Elaine told me she was going to take her stuffed Elvis bear with us on our honeymoon so he could go back home to Graceland. Elaine and I both laughed. I didn't think she was serious, as we used to joke around a lot. But when she unlatched her suitcase, it popped open and right there on top was Elvis Bear. I could not believe she really brought that stuffed bear with us.

The day we left the hotel for Graceland, Elaine had her Elvis bear tucked in her belt. She carried him with us all day long. While we were on the tour of Graceland, the guide would, from time to time, ask if anyone had any questions. Elaine had one. She asked if Priscilla ever got remarried after the divorce from Elvis. The guide said he did not know but would check with the other guides to see if any of them knew. We were almost at the end of the tour when the guide told our tour group that Priscilla never remarried. I quietly said to Elaine so no one could hear, "You knew that she never remarried. You just wanted everyone else to know too." Elaine just smiled.

After we got home, Elvis Bear was kept in our bedroom on top of our dresser mirror with other stuffed animals I bought her, usually for Valentine's Day. One Valentine's Day I gave her flowers and a purple stuffed bear. Elaine told me that this purple bear was going to be named Priscilla Presley. She wanted me to put it on top of the mirror beside Elvis Bear. Elaine asked me to do this for her because she was only five feet, two inches tall, so she could not reach some places. I told her that was not a good place to put the bear. She asked me why. I said, "Elvis and Priscilla did not get along well. After all, they were divorced!"

Elaine said, "Priscilla never remarried. Now put her up there beside Elvis." So I put Priscilla beside Elvis. Elaine gave me a kiss, and as she walked out of the room she said, "Priscilla is where she wanted to be, with Elvis."

All the years those two stuffed bears sat side by side, they never had one fight. So Elaine must have been right!

Parasailing

Elaine and I took a vacation to the city of Gulf Shores in Alabama. There were two reasons we picked this place. One was the ocean with a white-sand beach, because Elaine had never been to the ocean. I was born on the East Coast, so I grew up around the ocean, but I had not been to the beach in years. The second and main reason we picked this spot was that Elaine wanted to try parasailing. We both had a fear of heights, but Elaine wanted to overcome hers by parasailing over the Gulf Shore's blue ocean.

The day we went to the parasailing site, we were told it was the last day the company would be open for the season. Due to strong wind gusts, the captain was not sure if he was going to let anyone parasail. Just an hour earlier the winds had been too strong. Elaine still had not made up her mind as to whether she was going to go through with this.

She was walking around, talking with other parasailers. Some of the people were old pros, and some were first-timers like her. I was talking to the captain who told me that a week earlier, two parasailers were killed at another location due to wind gusts that made the parachute fold and the lines tangle. Less than thirty seconds after the captain told me this, Elaine came walking up to me and said, "I made up my mind, and I'm going to do it." I wanted to tell her, "No, you're not!" but she was smiling and looked so happy and excited that I did not say anything. I did not want to insist that she stay grounded and deprive her of something she wanted to experience.

Elaine ran off to sign her release form. I talked to the captain some more, and he could see I was worried. He told me that when we got out to sea, he would rely not just on the weather report, but also his experience. He said if anything looked dangerous, he would stop everything. We continued talking, and I got him to agree to make sure Elaine went up second. I wanted someone else to go up first to test things out.

Elaine did go second—she went four hundred feet up into the air. That was a happy and proud day for her. She told me that the next time we went someplace that had parasailing, she was going to go eight hundred feet high.

We stayed in a hotel with a beautiful beach, where every day we saw a dolphin swimming up and down the coastline. We also saw many other attractions in the area, but the highlight of our entire vacation was Elaine overcoming her fear of heights by parasailing.

Elaine's Lighthouses

Elaine was not the type of person who made demands of any kind on other people, so when she asked me to do something, I knew it was important to her. We had not been living in our country house very long—we still had some boxes that needed to be unpacked—when Elaine asked me to hang her lighthouse plaque on the wall.

I did not really think it was a big deal, but it made her happy because that plaque had a poem on it titled "Dreams." The plaque also had a picture of a lighthouse with waves crashing on the rocks below. Elaine told me that reading the poem had helped her through some tough times. The verse gave her strength to overcome her problems, and no matter how bad things seemed, they would get better. So both the picture and poem on the plaque were significant to her.

Elaine told me that whenever she saw a lighthouse, she pictured in her mind a ship fighting its way through a storm. She said the lighthouse was guiding the ship through the storm to safety. Elaine had weathered a lot of storms in her life. That is why she loved lighthouses.

Elaine had more hope than anyone I have ever met in my life. Someday I will see her in heaven. Until then, I will keep hope in my heart and live my life to make her proud.

I hope my story has helped you in some way. May God be with you, and may you find peace in your heart.

Acknowledgments

I WOULD LIKE TO THANK some special people in my life, without whose kind words, friendship, and encouragement this book would not have been possible.

Mary A. Deane, OP. Mary is an English teacher who gave me emotional support and encouragement, as well as helped me with the editing of my first draft. Mary has not only helped me on a professional level, but she has also become a very good friend. I appreciate everything she has done for me, and I am fortunate to have met her. Without Mary's help, this book would not have been possible. No words can truly express how grateful I am.

Robert Padberg, D. Min., Ph.D. Robert is a Pastoral Counselor and Clinical Psychologist. He has been a good friend and I have learned many things from him, especially how to [FROG], which means to [Fully Rely on God].

Sue A. Donlon. Sue is now retired, but she worked as a facilitator in many grief support groups. She was a grief counselor for seventeen years. I want to thank her for encouraging me to continue writing this book in spite of the obstacles I faced. I have dyslexia, so even though completing this book was important to me, there were many times I felt like giving up. I respect Sue's professional opinion; it meant a lot to me that she believed I could do this and thought there was value in what I was writing. Although I met her when I was

Acknowledgments

attending a grief support group and working through some issues, I consider her to be a friend and hope she is enjoying her retirement.

Kathy Flaherty. Kathy is a friend from the East Coast who talked with me in some of my darkest moments and who inspired me to keep hope in my heart. I am deeply thankful to her for motivating me to keep my dreams alive.

About the Author

MICHAEL THOMPSON was born in 1965 in Baltimore, Maryland. During his childhood years, his family resided in Brooklyn Park, Maryland, where he experienced big-city living. His family would occasionally take a weekend trip to Rehoboth Beach where he learned to appreciate and love the ocean.

Michael's family moved to Ohio in 1977. Once there, he joined the Korean Martial Arts Academy and became a black belt at age seventeen. As an adult, Michael became a correctional officer and worked in a state prison for twenty-one years.

Michael is now retired and spends time with his family and friends. He enjoys watching a good crime mystery, reading, writing, and relaxing at home. He still loves the ocean and enjoys visiting places where he can spend time on the beach.